PALAU

By Nancy Barbour
Edited By Mitchell P. Warner

Full Court Press
511 Mississippi
San Francisco, CA
9 4 1 0 7

Printed in Japan by Dai Nippon Printing Co.

Library of Congress Cataloging Publication No. 89-85-85112
ISBN: 0-9626344-0-9

At the time of publication, all information in this book was determined to be as accurate as
possible. Please be aware, however, that some hotels may have closed, some businesses may no longer
be functioning, and weather or other natural causes may have altered reef configurations.
The first aid information presented here is to help prevent or relieve suffering. While every reasonable
effort has been made to provide accurate information, no one involved with this book is
responsible for or assumes liability for any action taken by any person using information in this guide.
Anyone relying on the first aid presented in this book does so at his or her own risk.

Book Design by Nancy Barbour
Edited by Mitchell P. Warner
Copy Edited by Margo Paddock and Hazel White
Photo Credits:
Front Cover by Avi Klapfer
Back Cover:
Clownfish, Rick Tegeler; Starfish, Ed Robinson; Lionfish, Mitchell P. Warner

ACKNOWLEDGEMENTS

I met many wonderful people in Palau without whose help this book would not have been possible. My sincere appreciation goes to Shallum Etpison and his wife, Mandy, who generously offered the diving services of Neco Marine along with their warm friendship and hospitality. I especially want to thank Mandy for inspiring me to write this book in the first place. ¶ I would also like to thank Bena Sukuma for sharing his vast knowledge of the Palauan reefs and for giving me a greater insight to the Palauan people's love of their surrounding ocean. Thanks also to Johnny Kishigawa, Francis Toribiong, and Sam Whipps, who offered additional diving information. ¶ I am particularly grateful to Kempis Madd, who not only allowed me access to the Belau Museum's valuable collection of books but patiently endured my many questions about the Palauan legends. A special note of thanks goes to Joshua Koshiba for telling me the closely guarded family legend of the old woman of Ngercheu. I am also grateful to the group of women elders and others who related additional legends. ¶ I would also like to express my appreciation to Elaine de Man, who took the pitiful pages of what I thought was a manuscript and helped organize them into what she wisely knew was the first of many "first drafts." ¶ And special thanks goes to Mitch Warner of Guam. His comments as editor and words of support as a friend were invaluable. His knowledge of the Palauan reefs dates back to the beginning of sport diving in the islands in the early 1970s, and he was responsible for naming several of the dive sites. ¶ I would also like to thank my family and friends, who patiently tolerated my obsession with "the book" and my long periods of isolation. ¶ Special mention goes to George Balazs, Jeff La Douce, Al Giddings, Brian Gibeson, Avi Klapfer, Neil Montague, Ed Robinson, Sam Sargent, Rick Tegeler, and Mitchell P. Warner, whose exquisite photographs of Palau allow the beauty of these islands to come alive in the pages of this book. ¶ Finally, my heartfelt thanks goes to Dennis. Through our several years of friendship, he has not only showed me the wonders of the Palauan reefs, but taught me about the Palauan people as well. *Ke kmal mesaul.*

When I first visited Palau in December of
1986, I fell in love with it. I had never experienced the wonders of diving the Indo-Pacific Ocean,
and the islands were some of the most beautiful I had ever seen. When I left seven short days
later, I couldn't stop thinking about Palau. There were so many things I wanted to know, yet little
information was readily available. The islands are rich with history and the reefs are home to
many exotic creatures—some that are not known to exist anywhere else in the world. Yet few
visitors ever realize this.

I returned to Palau soon after my first visit with the intention of writing a dive guide.
Even considering all the beautiful diving I did while researching this book, some of the most
memorable moments were talking to the Palauan people about their legends. I became
increasingly intrigued with the sacred connection the Palaulans have to their surrounding
reefs—a connection that is revealed in many of their legends. I included the legends in this book
(several of which are here printed for the first time) to give the visitor a greater insight into the
fascinating history of Palau—a history that until recently was not written but passed on from
generation to generation in the form of stories.

Most of the legends that appear in these pages came from the Belau Museum. Many are
now preserved in storyboards, distinctive wood carvings that are for sale throughout Palau. A
portion of the legend "The Girl Who Turned Into a Dugong" is reprinted here with permis-
sion from the publisher of *Micronesian Customs and Beliefs,* by the Students of the Community
College of Micronesia, compiled and edited by Gene Ashby, revised edition published in
1985. The legend of "Uchelianged" was taken from a brochure from the Palau Pacific Resort.
Additional proverbs came from sayings collected by Robert K. McKnight with the help of

Adalbert Obak and Erminia Ngiraked reprinted in *Micronesian Research Working Papers*, John E. de Young, editor, published by the Office of the High Commissioner, Trust Territory of the Pacific Islands, 1966. The story that appears at the beginning of the diving section and the legend of Chandelier Cave were written by Mitchell P. Warner.

The Palauan people's strong sense of their traditional heritage and the influence of western society are apparent to the visitor immediately upon arrival in the islands. Many villages and dive sites have two names, the Palauan name and its English translation. Even the country itself is known by two names, *Palau* and the more traditional *Belau*. I have chosen to use the name *Palau* to identify the islands because it is more internationally recognized. In relating the legends, however, I have used the traditional name, *Belau*.

Nancy Barbour
1990

CONTENTS

MARIANAS
ISLANDS

$\mathcal{M} \quad I \quad C \quad R \quad O \quad N \quad E \quad S \quad I \quad A$

MARSHALL
ISLANDS

Palau
Islands

CAROLINE
ISLANDS

GILBERT
ISLANDS

HAWAII

The country of Belau, commonly known to the world as the Republic of Palau, is located on the western edge of Micronesia. Micronesia, a vast geographic area of the Pacific Ocean, consists of over 2,000 islands scattered between Hawaii and the Philippines. These islands are spread across an expanse of ocean the size of the continental United States, yet their combined land mass is only 1,055 square miles, roughly the size of the state of Rhode Island. There are four major island groups in Micronesia: the Marshalls, the Marianas, the Gilberts, and the Carolines. Palau is the westernmost island group of the Caroline archipelago, located approximately 600 miles east of the southernmost island of the Philippines and 400 miles north of the equator.

INTRODUCTION

In the most distant past, there were no people, there was no land. Uchelianged, the supreme Palauan god, looked down upon this vast ocean emptiness and said, "Let there arise a land." A volcanic rock arose from the sea upon which sat a giant clam. Its belly began to swell and tremble, and it grew larger and larger. But the clam was unable to give birth. Uchelianged saw this and said, "Let there be a strong running sea." The wind began to blow and waves crashed round the clam causing it finally to burst open, spewing forth swarms of the first sea creatures to swim the ocean. They in turn gave birth and the once empty seas were soon teeming with life, from the smallest sea worm to the grandest of human forms. And so Belau was born.

In the western Pacific Ocean, beginning just south of Japan, an underwater mountain range known as the Kyushu Ridge extends almost to the shores of New Guinea. Rising 27,000 feet from the ocean floor, the southernmost peaks of this vast mountain range form the islands of Palau.

A magnificent barrier reef surrounds most of these islands, creating one of the most spectacular diving areas in the world. The water, nearly as warm as the tropical air, is teeming with fish. Sheer vertical dropoffs start at the ocean's surface and plunge hundreds of feet. Miles and miles of reefs, many still unexplored, abound with exotic marine life. Underwater caves, blue holes, landlocked saltwater lakes, and Japanese shipwrecks from the Second World War offer a variety of diving sites rarely found in one area.

Preceding Page: The Rock Islands of Palau offer some of the most beautiful scenery in all of Micronesia. These islands, scattered throughout the central and southern part of Palau, are accessible only by boat. Photograph by Neil Montague. Photograph at left by Rick Tegeler

Early Palauan legends tell of the richness of these islands and so it is true today. There are more than 700 species of coral and over 1,000 species of fish. By comparison, Hawaii has roughly a third of these numbers. Brilliantly colored clownfish nestle among the stinging tentacles of anemones. Soft corals grace the reefs with their delicate colors. Manta rays and endangered hawksbill turtles glide through the clear water. And giant tridacna clams, some over three feet across and more than half a century old, lie in the shallow areas of the inner lagoon.

There are exotic marine animals in Palau that are rarely found in other parts of the world. The dugong, a marine mammal reduced to near extinction elsewhere, has managed to survive partly because ancient traditional law allowed the taking of dugongs only for Palauans of the highest rank. Saltwater crocodiles live in the mangrove swamps around the big island of Babeldaob and in some of the marine lakes in the famous Rock Islands. Palau is the only island group in Micronesia where crocodiles are found.

Crocodiles are not seen on the offshore reefs where most of the dive sites are located. Sharks, however, are a common sight—whitetips, blacktips, and grey reef sharks are the species most often encountered. Fortunately, they are not a threat to divers, for the surrounding waters offer an abundance of food. Although sharks are by nature unpredictable and deserve a healthy respect, the reef sharks that frequent the popular dive sites in Palau generally ignore divers and present little danger. Their unaggressive behavior makes them far more fascinating than frightening.

In addition to the exciting marine life, more than fifty ships from the Japanese Imperial Navy are lying on the bottom of the Palau Lagoon, casualties of the Second World War. Although many of these ships have been salvaged, there are several diveable wrecks that equal those of the famous Truk Lagoon. And for those who dream of discovering a virgin wreck, there are ships known to have sunk in Palau that have yet to be found. According to naval historian Samuel Eliot Morison, the American submarine *Tullibee* sank in the deep waters off the main channel on the western side of the islands. A Japanese ship loaded with flasks of mercury used for making explosives reportedly lies in the channel between the islands of Babeldaob and Koror. Palauan fishermen tell of a Spanish galleon off the southeastern shores of Angaur, and rumors persist of a sunken Japanese hospital ship laden with a secret cargo of gold.

Palau's enticing underwater scenery is equalled by a culture rich in folklore and legend. From these legends, several of which appear at the beginning of chapters throughout this book, much can be learned about the mysteries of these islands and their people.

With its fascinating culture, magnificent natural setting, and exotic marine life, Palau is a traveler's dream.

Palau's reefs are famous for their diverse marine life, which is due in part to the islands' proximity to the Indo-Malayan region. Most Pacific marine organisms evolved in the triangular area bounded by New Guinea, the Philippines, and the Malay Peninsula. As the distance from this area increases, the number of species decreases. Photograph by Avi Klapfer

GEOGRAPHY

Soon after the creation of the world, there was only one island. And on this island, which they called Angaur, there lived a child who was born of a giant clam. Her name was Uab and she was possessed of a voracious appetite. She ate so much and grew into such an enormous giant that the people of her village became threatened with famine. One night while she slept, they tied her up and set her ablaze. Uab roared and kicked and Angaur shook. The struggle was so fierce that she kicked herself into many pieces, large and small, which settled upon the ocean and formed the islands of Belau. The great bulk of her body became Babeldaob, the largest island. Her stomach rested in a village rich with food where the people eat seven times a day. Her vagina became a town that has the most rain in Belau, and where Uab's mouth settled, some say that the people talk too much.

Palau is an elongated chain of some 340 islands that stretch across 400 miles of ocean in a north-south direction. Only eight of the islands are inhabited. The population of the entire country is a mere 14,000 people, the majority of who live in the capital city of Koror. Most of Palau's 188 square miles of land is concentrated in a central cluster of islands that extends from the atoll of Kayangel in the north to Angaur in the south. Two hundred

Over the centuries, the Rock Islands have been transformed into distinctive shapes by a combination of physical and biological processes. As rainwater slowly seeps down through the rotting vegetation on the limestone islands, it becomes acidic. In calm weather this solution forms a floating lens of acidic water that surrounds the island and slowly eats away the limestone base. Further damage is caused by algae-eating marine organisms such as sea urchins, chitons, and limpets, which graze on the algae growing between the tidemarks on the limestone base.

miles farther south and stretching across yet another 200 miles of ocean toward New Guinea are five small isolated islands collectively known as the Southwest Islands. Even though these islands are technically a part of Palau, the inhabitants, all seventy-seven of them, speak a dialect more similar to the neighboring Caroline Islands.

Palau is famous for its breathtaking coral reefs, but the scenery above water is just as spectacular. The island geology is unique, for rarely do you find such diverse formations in close proximity. The volcanic island of Babeldaob, the second largest island in Micronesia, rises over 700 feet above sea level and hosts inland waterfalls surrounded by lush tropical rain forests. In contrast, the four low-lying islands of Kayangel sit atop a limestone reef growing from the rim of a submerged volcano. These islands now form a coral atoll that rises but a few feet above sea level. With deserted white sand beaches and a shallow turquoise lagoon, Kayangel fits the classic western image of a tropical island paradise.

The southern islands of Peleliu and Angaur are limestone reef flats that were uplifted by volcanic forces. The land is now riddled with deep caves and natural crevices. During World War II, Japanese forces used these caves to construct an intricate system of passages and underground fortifications that went undetected by American aerial reconnaissance. The Americans mistakenly thought the island could be easily taken, but the battle turned into one of the bloodiest of the Pacific war. It took over 2,000 tons of explosives before the American flag flew over Peleliu.

But the most fascinating geological formations in Palau are the Rock Islands—the scenic highlight of all Micronesia. These islands, scattered throughout the central and southern part of the Palauan archipelago, are the remains of ancient coral reefs uplifted by volcanic forces millions of years ago. Some tower several hundred feet above the ocean and are covered with dense jungle, yet others are barely large enough to support a single coconut tree. All have been undercut at the waterline by centuries of erosion and algae-eating marine organisms, giving them the appearance of giant emerald mushrooms. Fringing the shores of many of these uninhabited islands are secluded sand beaches backed by nearly impenetrable jungle. Cockatoos, parrots, and fruit bats—an endangered fruit-eating, flying mammal—soar among the towering palm trees.

Hidden within the interiors of some of the larger Rock Islands are mysterious saltwater lakes, each connected to the surrounding ocean by underground tunnels that vary in size from small fissures to openings large enough to swim through. Each lake is unique, with its own physical, chemical, and biological properties. The water temperature in one lake is over 100° F just fifteen feet below the surface. Another lake is populated almost entirely by a species of jellyfish found nowhere else in the world, and still another supports a complete tropical reef community including sharks and an occasional transient saltwater crocodile.

One tightly clustered, isolated group of Rock Islands known as the Seventy Islands was designated as a wildlife preserve by the Palauan government in 1956. Today it is a well-known nesting ground for two endangered species, the hawksbill turtle and the Micronesian megapode, a gull-sized, ground-dwelling bird that makes nests as large as fifteen feet across. The Seventy Islands form a protected environment for much of Palau's wildlife, and by law no one is allowed on the islands. Sadly, lack of money for enforcement often results in poaching.

Not only is the scenery of Palau as beautiful as it is diverse, but the islands themselves are full of mystery and intrigue. Angered spirits of the ancestral dead are thought to roam through the islands at night. Giant stone faces, their origins unknown, lie scattered about Melekeok village on the island of Babeldaob. Ancient rock paintings adorn the inaccessible cliffs of Ulong Island, and the unexplained remains of the sunken village of Ngiptal lie just off the eastern shore of Babeldaob—all adding an air of adventure to a spectacular natural setting.

CULTURE

The giant body of the fallen Uab lay exposed for days and days. Finally, the people of her village decided to cover her with mats. But Uab's body was of such great size that there were not enough mats, so branches had to be used as well. Even the branches and mats could cover only half her body. And so today the Belau Islands are half forest and half plains. And the worms that were born from Uab's rotted body became the people of Belau.

No one really knows where the original Palauans came from. Current western theory, based on linguistic similarities, holds that Palau was settled by people from northern Indonesia and the Philippines who sailed hundreds of miles across open ocean 2,000 to 3,000 years before the birth of Christ. However, this theory is still debated.

The early Palauans lived in isolation from the outside world. With the abundance of food from their fertile islands and surrounding reefs, there was little need to explore beyond their shores. The men were excellent fishermen and had a greater understanding of the complex ocean currents and life cycles of fish than is known in western society even today. The women were equally skilled in agriculture, primarily in the growing of taro, a staple food crop whose tuberous roots are rich in protein. Women took great pride in the cultivation of their taro patches, a well-tended garden was the foremost criterion by which women judged their peers. Since many patches were located in one common field, women worked side by side and were able to compare and compete with one another in the size of roots and the abundance of the harvest.

Because the men were freed from the time-consuming and physically demanding task of farming, they were able to devote their energies to refining other skills. Aside from fishing, the men spent much of their time constructing village buildings, making dugout canoes, and carving elaborate wooden bowls, plates, and large, intricate food containers that they inlaid with shell. But the most outstanding example of their craftsmanship was the *bai*, a gathering place for the men of the village. The *bai*, a high-peaked structure made of wood and thatch, was a masterpiece of Micronesian architecture. Built from large, heavy planks of wood that were felled and carved without metal tools, the structure was held together by nothing more than the precise fit of the wooden beams. Carved and painted stories depicting Palauan legends, humorous tales, and historic events of the village decorated the interior beams and outside gables. The most elaborately constructed *bai* functioned as a meeting place or council house for the governing elders of the village. Other *bais* served as gathering places for the men of the community where the traditional skills of fishing, hunting, carving, and carpentry were learned.

Rivaling the *bai* in beauty of craftsmanship was the Palauan sailing canoe, the *kaeb*, slim of line and built for speed. The average *kaeb* was thirty-three feet long, yet its beam was a mere fourteen inches. Early German ethnographers report that the *kaeb* was even faster than the famous "flying proa" from the Caroline Islands, a canoe that many consider the fastest ever made but one that Palauans mockingly referred to as a "dish."

Equally as impressive as the *kaeb* was the giant war canoe, a paddling canoe often as long as sixty feet and able to hold as many as thirty-two warriors. Both the *kaeb* and the war canoe were single-hulled outrigger designs, carved from the trunk of a single tree.

The early Palauans developed a complex and highly organized social system that today mystifies all but the most dedicated anthropologists. In a matrilineal system, which still exists, nuclear families and extended families, called clans, were related through the mother's side of the family. About one in four children was adopted, and the mother's brother had a greater role than the natural father in providing for the children. Money, in the form of beads made from a stone that is not known to exist in Palau, was used in a complex system of exchange in which each individual piece was named and its previous clan owners known. This money continues to be used today in certain traditional marriage and childbirth ceremonies.

Over the years the culture has been slowly changing to meet the needs of a developing nation. Today the outboard motor has replaced the sailing canoe, much of the ancient fishing knowledge has been lost, nearly seventy-five percent of the work force is employed by the government, and Coke cans now appear alongside coconuts in grocery store coolers. But the Palauans are a proud people with a strong sense of heritage, and many ancient traditions remain. Women still tend the village taro gardens, and hereditary chiefs continue to exert considerable influence in political decisions even though the country now elects its government officals. Both men and women chew betel nut, a green palm nut sprinkled with tobacco and powdered lime—lime powder that is made by heating coral rocks over a slow burning fire until the limestone is reduced to powder. The entire concoction is then wrapped in a leaf from a pepper tree. When chewed, it produces a narcotic effect that cools the body and turns the teeth red.

The ancient carvings that appeared on the *bai* have evolved into storyboards, carved planks of wood depicting colorful Palauan legends that have become popular souvenirs. Today storyboards are carved primarily by prison inmates. As a result, the jail, with its corrugated tin sheds and dirt yard, is one of the most popular tourist attractions in Koror.

HISTORY

*Long ago the people from
the small island of Yap had nothing in their islands from
which to make money. So they traveled the long
journey to Belau in outrigger canoes, and there among the
Rock Islands they found a rare stone—a limestone that was
strong yet soft enough to be carved. At first they carved
the rock into the shape of a shark, the brave fish of the
sea. The shape was good but the length was too long and this
made the money brittle. After many other failed attempts
they grew tired. Darkness fell and the moon rose large
and bright. It was then that they knew what they should
do. With their adze tools they carved the rock into large
round shapes and made a hole in the center. Thus they could
carry the pieces on a pole and load them in canoes to be
sailed back across the sea to their home islands of Yap.*

The islands of Palau remained virtually unknown to the western world during the first two centuries of European exploration in the Pacific. After Magellan's successful circumnavigation of the world in 1519, Spanish ships entered the Pacific with orders to explore, conquer, and colonize in the name of God and the king of Spain. Trade routes between Spain's New World port of Alcapulco and the Spanish settlement in the Philippines were established, and Manila galleons laden with precious gems, silks, spices, and teas from the orient, as well as freshly minted silver from Mexico, were an annual sight in

Although most foreign explorers were unaware of the Palau Islands, the people of Yap routinely made the 500-mile round-trip journey to Palau in outrigger canoes to quarry their enormous pieces of money. This money, the largest in the world, often measured ten to twelve feet in diameter and was carved from the unique limestone of Palau's Rock Islands. Not all of the money made it back to Yap, however. This nearly completed piece is hidden in the jungles of Babeldaob. Photograph by Mitchell P. Warner

the Pacific between 1565 and 1815. By the end of the seventeenth century, Spain had laid claim to much of Micronesia. Even though Palau lay south of the galleon trade routes, at least seven expeditions were made around Palau during this time. Yet none of the explorers happened to find the Palauan Islands.

Some historians believe that the Spaniard Ruy Lopez de Villalobos was the first European to locate Palau in his voyage of 1543. Others believe that the English privateer, Sir Francis Drake, landed in the islands in 1579. But evidence supporting each of these claims is inconclusive.

In fact, European explorers were not able to find Palau until somebody told them where to look. In 1696 a canoe of fishermen from a small island in the Western Carolines landed in a Spanish settlement in the Philippines after being blown hundreds of miles off course by a storm. The fishermen made a crude map of their home islands, stimulating the interest of Jesuit missionaries, who envisioned undiscovered lands perhaps rich in gold or silver but certainly populated by thousands of heathen souls in need of salvation.

In 1710 a ship under the command of Don Francisco Padilla left the Philippines in search of the new lands. It arrived at the small Palauan island of Sonsorol, which lies several hundred miles south of the main Palau group, and two missionaries went ashore to raise the cross. The missionaries were never heard from again.

Undaunted, Padilla continued to sail north and soon landed at the main Palau archipelago. As he was dropping anchor, several Palauans boarded his ship. Believing that anything that arrived in the islands was rightfully theirs, the Palauans began removing everything they could, especially bits of iron. Shots were fired by the Spanish, spears were thrown by the Palauans, and Padilla quickly pulled anchor. Thus the first documented contact between Europeans and Palauans was written into the pages of history.

Little is known about further foreign contact until 1783, when British Captain Henry Wilson wrecked his ship, the *Antelope,* on the western reefs of Palau near Koror. Wilson and his crew were able to salvage some supplies and row to the nearby uninhabited island of Ulong, where they spent three months rebuilding their ship with the help and support of Chief Ibedul of Koror. So strong a friendship developed between the two leaders that on the day of Wilson's departure he was honored with the highest distinction in Palau—a bracelet made from the vertebrae of a dugong was ceremonially placed on his wrist. In appreciation Wilson gave Ibedul guns, a previously unknown weapon among the warring tribes of Palau. These gifts were to have a great effect upon the subsequent balance of power among the villages of Palau.

Wilson's experiences helped open the islands to further foreign contact, and over the next one hundred years Palau saw an influx of British traders, American whalers, and German merchants. Not only did these visitors introduce deadly contagious diseases, reducing Palau's population from 40,000 to 4,000 by the 1900s, but their presence also threatened Spain's hold on the islands. Finally in 1885 Pope Leo XIII was called in as an arbitrator, ultimately upholding Spain's 300-year-old claim to Micronesia.

The Spanish-American War marked the end of Spain as a Pacific power. In 1899 Spain sold Palau together with the Carolines, the Marshalls, and the Northern Marianas (with the exception of Guam) to Germany. Guam, the largest island in the Marianas chain, was purchased by the United States.

Germany's main interest in Palau was economic. Phosphate, a substance derived from bird droppings and valued as fertilizer, was mined on the island of Angaur. In addition, coconut plantations were set up throughout the islands to expand Germany's profitable trade in copra, the dried meat of the coconut from which oil is extracted. During the latter part of the nineteenth century, a shortage of dairy fats in northern Europe created a great demand for copra as an alternative source of edible fat.

Germany's control of Palau lasted only fifteen years. Japan seized the islands in 1914 at the beginning of World War I and remained in power for the next thirty years. Japan expanded the commercial ventures started by the Germans and built a thriving economy based on phosphate mining, commercial fishing, and the farming of rice, pineapples, and coconuts. Schools were built, roads paved, and sewer systems developed.

Koror became the administrative center for Japan's Pacific empire. Japanese were encouraged to emigrate to Palau, and they soon outnumbered the Palauans four to one. It was during this period that the Palauan culture saw its most dramatic change. There was a shift in power from village chiefs to Japanese administrators. Koror became a stylish oriental metropolis with public baths, gourmet restaurants, and geishas.

During the 1930s Japan began fortifying the islands as an imperial outpost. By 1938 Palau was a closed military area. Ironically, a country that took hundreds of years for foreign explorers to find was now located in an area of immense strategic importance.

In 1944 American forces, in their push toward the Philippines and their final invasion of Japan, were convinced that Palau was a logical stepping stone. Their main target was the airfield on the island of Peleliu. With little accurate intelligence, the Americans believed that the island was flat and could be easily taken. In reality, the land is composed of elevated limestone ridges riddled with natural caves, which had been heavily fortified by the Japanese. When American forces stormed the island on September 15th, they were faced with a rugged terrain of dense jungle, peaks rising over 200 feet, ground made of jagged coral rocks sharp enough to cut through the soles of shoes, and an enemy ready and willing to fight until death. The fighting lasted nearly three months. At one point American forces controlled the surface, but the entrenched Japanese were underneath their feet, and there was no way to dislodge them. The battle at Peleliu was one of the toughest, bloodiest operations of the Pacific war. An estimated 11,000 Japanese and 1,000 Americans lost their lives.

World War II shattered Palau. Caught in the cross fire between Japanese and American forces, Palauans were the victims of events over which they had no control. Food was in short supply, medical care was minimal, schools were closed, trade ruined. As a result, traditional Palauan authority began to re-emerge, and a strong anti-foreign reaction developed. At the end of World War II, the United States took control of a physically destroyed nation and a people eager for self-government.

In 1947 Palau as well as the rest of Micronesia, with the exception of Guam, became a trust territory of the United Nations administered by the U.S. government, first under the authority of the navy, and after 1962 under the Department of the Interior. Known as the U.S. Trust Territory of the Pacific Islands, the area was eventually divided into four political districts; the Commonwealth of the Northern Marianas, the Federated States of Micronesia, the Republic of the Marshall Islands, and the Republic of Palau. Three of the four territories have negotiated agreements with the United States—the Northern Marianas are now a commonwealth; the Marshall Islands and the Federated States of Micronesia are now self-governing nations with the United States responsible for defense. The Palauans, however, adopted a constitution in 1981 that contained certain provisions unacceptable to the American government. At issue was one provision declaring Palau a nuclear-free zone, a position at odds with the United States' intentions of basing nuclear weapons on the islands as well as possibly establishing a military base as part of its defense strategy. If an agreement between the two governments—known as the Compact of Free Association—is approved, Palau will become a self-governing nation and the United States will be responsible for defense and for providing agreed upon amounts of economic and service assistance. But after years of negotiation and many votes by the Palauan people, a stalemate between the two countries still exists. As of the date of this publication, Palau has the dubious distinction of being the world's sole remaining trust territory.

DIVING

There once was an underwater photographer who came to Palau and began asking everyone he met, "When is the best time to dive?" Three different divers gave three different answers—the taxi driver had a fourth opinion and the waiter had another. Over dinner the eager photographer sought out other divers for their ideas of when and where was the best place to dive. Each person expounded at length on his favorite sites and theories, with no two being alike. The frustrated photographer finally found an old fisherman who was known throughout the islands for his knowledge of the ocean. When questioned as to a system for finding the best visibility and the most fish, the wise old man gazed out into the sea and slowly responded, "It is the Ocean. It is not predictable."

The maximum speed limit on the streets of Palau is a leisurely 25 mph. Palauans make up for this when they get behind the wheel of a boat. The dive boats are equipped with powerful twin outboard motors capable of over 35 knots. Even at these speeds, the dive sites are anywhere from twenty minutes to an hour away from Koror, but the scenery along the way is spectacular and time passes quickly.

Dive operators normally offer daylong excursions with two tank dives. Boats leave the docks in Koror at 9:00 a.m. and generally return no later than 4:00 p.m. There is a two-hour surface interval between dives, which is generally spent on a secluded beach, eating, snorkeling, exploring, or just relaxing.

Preceding page: Some of the most spectacular dropoffs in Palau are located around the Ngemelis Islands along the southwestern barrier reef. This area is known for its sheer vertical walls that drop nearly 1,000 feet and the shallow reef tops that grow to within several feet of the surface. Photograph by Mitchell P. Warner

The return trip to Koror often takes you through the beautiful Rock Islands, an uninhabited, complex maze of islands that only a knowledgeable few can navigate. Winding through shallow lagoons with the wind in your hair and coral inches below your feet, and passing within a whisper of an undercut limestone island is an adventure in itself and an exciting way to end a day of diving.

Palau is famous for its spectacular vertical reefs, most of which drop hundreds of feet yet grow to within twenty feet of the surface. Divers can dive any depth they choose and are responsible for their own bottom time and safety. There are dive guides on each boat, but they don't always stay with the group during the dive. Pre-dive briefings are exactly that—brief. "Keep the wall on your right" is often the only information that you will receive. Experienced divers will love the freedom; those wanting more supervision may want to team up with more experienced divers. You can ask the guides to stay with you during the dive, but don't count on their constant presence.

The clear waters and near-vertical dropoffs make deep dives tempting. Be aware that not all of the dive boats carry oxygen for treatment of the bends. Even though there is a one-man recompression chamber at the hospital in Koror, it is a lousy way to spend an afternoon.

All diving in Palau is drift diving. The current carries you along the edge of the reef, and the boat picks you up wherever you surface at the end of the dive. The average current is a manageable one-half knot, but on occasion it gets stronger, making it difficult to stop along the wall to take photographs. During these times it is best just to enjoy the ride. Sailing along a beautiful coral wall with little or no effort is a thrill that is hard to beat.

Because of the currents, minimal supervision, and deep vertical dropoffs, the dive sites along the outer barrier reef are not recommended for novice divers. Trips for less experienced scuba divers can be arranged, however, and there are beautiful shallow areas around the Rock Islands for snorkeling. For example, one of the largest concentrations of soft coral in Palau grows in just twenty feet of water in an arch between two rock islands. A Japanese Zero fighter plane in near-perfect condition lies in ten feet of water on the eastern side of Palau, and giant tridacna clams, some over three feet across and weighing more than several hundred pounds, live in the shallow waters off a few Rock Island beaches.

You can request any type of diving you want, within reason, and for a price. Perhaps you would rather make three dives a day instead of the usual two or dive once in the morning and spend the afternoon on a secluded beach. You can make special arrangements to dive the pristine reefs of the southernmost island of Angaur or arrange a two-day trip to the beautiful northern atoll of Kayangel, which includes camping under the stars on an uninhabited island.

There is a motel on Carp Island, just twenty minutes from the popular dive sites of the Ngemelis area in southern Palau, with private bungalows and a resident staff who will prepare meals. You can also spend the week on a live-aboard dive boat. All of these arrangements can be made with dive or tour operators and are just a few of the many choices available.

The diving season in Palau is year-round. Winds are less likely to affect the more popular dive sites along the western barrier reef from January to June, and there are fewer chances of heavy rain showers during these months. But no matter what time of year you visit Palau, there are always places to dive because of the variety of locations around the islands.

Water temperatures remain constant throughout the year, averaging 84° F. Visibility ranges from fifty to 150 feet along the outer barrier reef and is greatly influenced by the daily tides and weather. Visibility within the confined water of the inner lagoon where most of the shipwrecks are located averages thirty to sixty feet. As a general rule, the water is clearest along the outer barrier reef during the final two hours of an incoming tide. Schools of pelagic fish are often more abundant when the current is strong. Reef fish usually feed most actively at the beginning of incoming and outgoing tides, although the height of the tides, wind direction, seasonal migrations, phases of the moon, and many other factors influence behavior. The dive sites are different every day and every time you dive them, continually offering the thrill of the unexpected. Dive operators make every effort to select the best dive sites to take advantage of changing conditions.

The size and type of boats used for diving in Palau varies, but most can accommodate between six and twelve divers. Many of the boats are uncovered, so a tight-fitting hat, sunglasses, and sunscreen are strongly recommended. You will need diving booties or some type of rubber-soled shoes for walking from the boat to the beach during lunch. Also, a lightweight nylon windbreaker is a welcome relief when it rains.

Dive shops have rental equipment available and dive equipment is for sale in several stores, but most divers who come to Palau bring all of their own gear, including wetsuits. Even in these warm waters, many divers like to wear a lightweight wetsuit or Lycra bodysuit for warmth as well as for protection from stinging hydroids. Dive operators provide tanks, weight belts, and weights.

Photographers should bring their own film and batteries. Although you can buy these items in Koror, you can't depend on the stores to always have in stock the kind of film or batteries you need. There is a twenty-four-hour print film developing service in town, but slide processing services are not available to date, and there are no camera repair shops.

With over fifty identifiable dive sites in Palau and more being discovered each year, it is difficult to describe them all. But every world-class dive area becomes known for a few of its spectacular sites. The following pages describe several of those that have given Palau its excellent reputation.

After a morning dive along the barrier reef, divers often stop for lunch at one of the many isolated beaches that fringe the shores of the Rock Islands in southern Palau. Photograph by Rick Tegeler

SIAES TUNNEL

*N*gkora killii a Derudm
el medela betok el tekoi—"Like one who has eaten
the spiny puffer fish, full of many things."
If a large mouthed grouper eats the spiny puffer fish,
which has thorns covering its entire body, the puffer, in
self-defense, will expand and send his thorns through
the soft flesh of the grouper's mouth. The grouper, "full of
many things," is entirely helpless. Belauans use this proverb
to characterize someone who gets into more trouble than
he can handle, be it money, work, or women.

Siaes (pronounced Si-EZ) Tunnel is an enormous underwater cavern that cuts through a corner of Palau's western barrier reef, just northwest of Ulong Island. The depth of the tunnel varies from an eighty-foot ceiling to a 130-foot bottom, so it is best to be prepared for a 110- to 120-foot dive. There is enough natural light inside the cavern to make the dive without a light, but if you have one, bring it—the colors of the sponges and corals that encrust the walls of the cave come alive in artificial light.

The dive begins at the edge of a dropoff in fifteen feet of water and continues down a vertical coral-covered wall to the entrance to the tunnel. There are actually three entrances, one at each end and a small window opening in the middle. Because the tunnel cuts through the reef at an angle, the entrance on the north side of the corner is the shallowest of the three, ranging

Soft corals, <u>Dendronephthya sp.</u>, are some of the most beautiful corals on the reef. Their soft, translucent bodies vary in shades of pink, purple, orange, and red. These animals prefer areas of moderate current, where they can feed on plankton by extending their tentacles into the flowing water. When the current slows, the polyps retract and await the rhythmic flow of water to begin again. Photograph by Ed Robinson

from eighty to one hundred feet. But entering the tunnel through the huge gaping hole on the south side of the corner is more exciting. It's deeper (ninety to 130 feet) and darker, but far more dramatic. Entering a dimly lit cavern at one hundred feet, swimming among towering bushes of black coral, and exiting through seven-foot sea fans exquisitely backlit from the outside light is as thrilling as it is beautiful.

The small window opening in the middle of the tunnel at a depth of ninety feet is one of the most peaceful places on the reef. Surrounded by a garden of sea fans and soft corals, it is a gorgeous area for photography or for just gazing out into 600 miles of open ocean. Reef sharks often cruise along this wall, and at times you can see the silhouette of a graceful manta ray in the distance.

Siaes Reef forms the northern tip of a large horseshoe-shaped underwater bay that juts far out into the prevailing currents of the Philippine Sea. Consequently, big open-ocean fish such as wahoo and tuna are often found in this area. Even marlin, a popular game fish rarely seen by divers, have been spotted.

Because of its depth, the Siaes Tunnel is recommended for experienced divers. For those who don't feel like exploring the deep tunnel, the wall itself is an exceptional dive. Hundreds of pyramid butterflyfish, a brightly colored black and yellow fish common on the outer reefs of Palau, hover along the edge of the dropoff, and large sea fans and delicate soft corals decorate the vertical face of the wall.

In 1783 British Captain Henry Wilson played a significant role in the history of Palau when his ship, the *Antelope*, ran aground on the reef several miles north of Siaes Tunnel. Wilson and his crew were able to salvage lifeboats and supplies and row to nearby Ulong Island, where they spent three months rebuilding their ship. Prior to this time, little had been known about Palau, and Wilson's experiences helped open the islands to further Western contact. Today dive boats often stop at Ulong Island after a morning dive at Siaes.

Bring your camera; this is one of the most beautiful beaches in Palau.

Interestingly enough, Siaes Tunnel was discovered by accident. As the story goes, a group of divers was on its way to a dive site a little north of this area. The pace of the islands being what it is, the dive guide didn't quite feel up to going the extra distance and instead dropped his group along an unexplored area of the reef. As they descended the vertical wall, they came upon the huge cavern at one hundred feet. The beauty and excitement of this previously unknown area give some indication of the underwater secrets that may still be hidden along the miles of unexplored reefs surrounding Palau.

SHARK CITY

*N*gkora ngkelel a
iusuch el dimengela medad rengii— "Like fish in deep,
clear water, eaten only with the eyes."
Palauans use this saying when referring to things
that can be only admired, like expensive items in a store
or another's wife.

Shark City is a wild place. You never know what to expect. In spite of the name, you might see but one lone shark swimming off in the distance. This area was once known for schools of aggressive grey reef sharks that at times prevented divers from even getting in the water. Today individual reef sharks are still found in this area, but large schools of sharks are rarely seen.

Shark City is located along Palau's western barrier reef, just southwest of Ulong Island. Unlike most other dropoffs in Palau, which begin within several feet of the surface, the top of this reef starts at a depth of fifty feet. A large ravine cuts into the near-vertical face of the wall, and table corals, six to eight feet in diameter, cover the reef flat. These corals provide shelter for a host of interesting creatures, including lobsters, crinoids, and nocturnal basket stars whose long, delicate arms are wound into tight balls during the day. Even the rare golden cowry, which by day generally hides deep within the coral, has been found by local fishermen when spear fishing along this deep, exposed dropoff at night.

The Napoleon wrasse, Cheilinus undulatus, *is one of the largest of all reef fish. Although they can grow to seven feet and weigh over 400 pounds, the ones most often seen in Palau are generally three to four feet long. Despite its size, the Napoleon wrasse is very wary and difficult to approach. Adults often develop a prominent bump on their foreheads—hence the common name, humphead wrasse.* Photograph by Rick Tegeler

This area is known for its large reef fish, from the big bumphead parrot, spotted triggerfish, and twenty-pound red snapper to the enormous Napoleon wrasse, one of the largest of all reef fish, capable of growing to 400 pounds.

Shark City forms the southern end of a large horseshoe-shaped underwater bay. Like Siaes Reef, which forms the bay's northern tip, Shark City juts far out into the prevailing currents of the Philippine Sea. As a result open-ocean fish are often sighted. A resident school of barracuda numbering in the hundreds patrols this area when the feeding opportunities are good, as do wahoo, yellowfin tuna, and other deep-water fish.

The big pelagics seem to swim farther away from the reef here compared with the other dive sites in Palau, where they come in right next to the dropoff. If you swim away from the wall into the blue water of the open ocean, pay attention to your depth—when the current is strong, you may encounter down-wellings. This is often the second dive of the day so many divers stay on top of the reef in fifty to sixty feet of water and watch the medley of fish swim by.

The emperor angelfish, Pomacanthus imperator, is just one of the many colorful tropical reef fish found in Palau. Photograph by Rick Tegeler

BLUE HOLES

*In Belau the sun is said to
follow a winding path through the sky until in early
evening it alights in an orange tree. Before making its final
descent into the western sea, it hurls the fruit into the
ocean in order to frighten away the sharks. As the fruit hits
the water, soft flashes of reds and yellows are seen on the
horizon as the sun safely settles for the night.*

At some unknown time in geological history, after strong currents and storm waves had crashed against Palau's western barrier reef for centuries, a great underwater cavern was formed. Gradually over the ages, parts of its ceiling gave way, creating four vertical shafts, or blue holes, that open to the surface above. In time low-light reef organisms settled in its dark recesses, and the cave became a haven for rays, turtles, large groupers, and sleeping sharks. Today divers can explore this vast underwater formation, awed by the powerful natural forces that created the Blue Holes.

A short snorkel across the shallow reef top to one of the four chimney entrances is hardly preparation for the eighty-foot free-fall through the body of the reef. As you slowly descend to this cathedral-like chamber, light diffuses through the spectrum of soft greens to sapphire blues, and disappears to indigo below. From the near spiritual setting created by the rays of sunlight filtering down through the vertical shafts to the intrigue of exploring the interior caves and crevices, this unique underwater chamber transcends the mundane surface world.

Rays of sunlight filter down through vertical shafts of the Blue Holes and bathe this immense underwater cavern in rich, warm light, providing a dramatic setting for available light photography. Photograph by Rick Tegeler

Solitary wire corals, some over thirty feet long, hang from the ceiling of the cave, and whitetip reef sharks occasionally sleep on the sandy 110-foot bottom of the cavern. At eighty feet a large, arched passage framed with black coral opens to a deep dropoff. Below this exit a sandy area spills out from the floor of the cavern where bottom-dwelling leopard sharks, a species similar in appearance to nurse sharks but unique to the Indo-Pacific, are sometimes seen.

There are a number of blue holes in Palau, but the most popular to dive is the group of four holes located along the southwestern barrier reef, just west of the Ngemelis Islands (pictured in the center of the aerial photograph at right). The large reef peninsula above the Blue Holes is Blue Corner, a dive site famous for its numerous sharks and large schools of pelagic fish. Photograph by Ed Robinson

BLUE CORNER

*A*rengalk el sechal a
dimekekerei ekora mersaod el mel bard er tir ra btil
a ralm—"The male child, though small, is like the small
barracuda that braces against the flowing water."
The small barracuda, mersaod, holds steady against the
current as it rushes off the reef. Suddenly it attacks a small fish
and just as quickly returns to its place of quiet observation.
This watchful, patient, almost crafty approach to life
is much admired in Belau, and parents use this proverb
to teach their male children.

Blue Corner is the place to dive if you want to see sharks, lots of them. Whitetips, blacktips, and grey reef sharks are a common sight along this area of the southwestern barrier reef. In addition to the near-constant parade of sharks, the resident school of barracuda, which numbers easily over five hundred, has made Blue Corner the most popular dive site in Palau.

Blue Corner is located on the tip of an underwater peninsula that turns a ninety-degree angle, forming an actual corner that juts far out into the open ocean. An exciting phenomenon occurs along this reef during an incoming tide. As the incoming current hits the deep, vertical wall, nutrient-rich water rushes toward the surface, causing a chain reaction in the feeding cycle: small fish leave the shelter of the reef to feed on the current-borne nutrients, large fish move up from the deeper areas of the dropoff. Schools of pelagic fish sweep in from the open ocean in search of prey, and grey reef sharks silently patrol the edge of the dropoff. A Palauan dive operator explains this phenom-

Grey reef sharks, Carcharhinus amblyrhynchos, are a common sight at Blue Corner. In the distance a graceful manta ray swims by. Photograph by Ed Robinson

enon best: "The little fish comes out, the big fish comes up, the bigger fish comes in, and the sharks are feeding on the rest."

A typical dive begins at the edge of the dropoff in twenty feet of water. Divers then drift toward the corner of the reef along a vertical wall that drops more than 1,000 feet. "Keep the wall on your right and the sharks on your left," as one dive guide explains. There is no need to swim away from the dropoff to see the big fish since they come in right next to the reef. You can dive any depth you choose, but most divers stay between fifty and eighty feet to maximize their bottom time.

The current is generally strong at the corner, but since this is where most of the fish are, many divers grab onto a rock at the edge of the dropoff and watch the show.

Schools of iridescent blue fusiliers pour down the reef like flowing waterfalls while hundreds of pyramid butterflyfish flutter along the edge of the dropoff. Schools of jacks, snapper, and surgeonfish swarm in the confusion as grey reef sharks, sometimes twenty strong, majestically glide through the open water just beyond the edge of the dropoff.

The sharks at Blue Corner are far more interested in fish than in divers and are amazingly unaggressive. Although all sharks can be unpredictable and should be regarded with caution, here is a rare opportunity to see these magnificent creatures in relative safety.

The enormous school of three-foot barracuda often stalks the corner of the reef. At times the school moves away from the dropoff when divers are in the water and hovers just within the limits of visibility, forming its own shim-

---

The resident school of barracuda, Sphyraena genus, forms a flowing sculpture of silver fish. Barracuda are large, voracious predators with needlelike teeth that protrude from their lower jaw, giving them a menacing look. They feed on small fish in the open water and are masters in making themselves invisible to their prey. When seen head-on their narrow profile looks small and unalarming so they can approach their prey unnoticed and attack with a sudden lunge. Photograph by Avi Klapfer

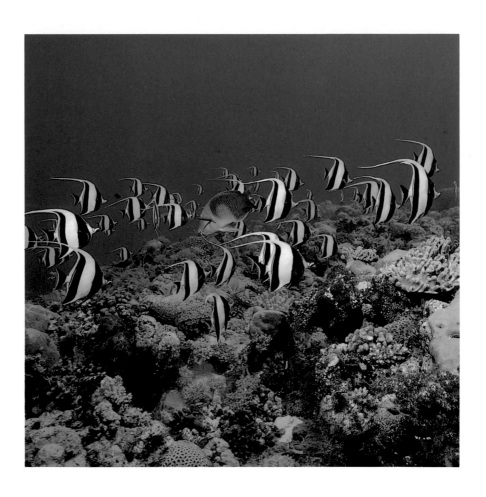

mering silver wall. Sometimes the school will split into smaller groups and cautiously swim back over the top of the reef. These barracuda have never been known to attack divers, and their wary behavior suggests that they are far more frightened by you than you are by them.

This is an exceptional reef, but its beauty almost goes unnoticed because of all the fish. Giant sea fans and massive stands of black coral adorn the dropoff at eighty feet. Gardens of soft corals grow along the vertical face of the wall. Anemones and colorful clownfish are abundant, and hawksbill turtles are occasionaly seen. A vast field of garden eels lives in the sand rivers on top of the reef at the corner, challenging even the most seasoned underwater photographer.

Blue Corner is full of surprises—every dive offers something new and different. Even the most jaded divers are amazed by the variety of marine life. Because the current can be strong along this reef, Blue Corner is recommended for experienced divers.

A school of delicate Moorish idols, <u>Zanclus cornutus</u>, swims along the top of the reef at Blue Corner. Moorish idols generally feed in groups of four or five—rarely are they seen in schools this large. At certain times of the year, possibly during their spawning season, large aggregations of Moorish idols can be seen in other areas of Palau as well, but the school at Blue Corner is generally present throughout the year. Photograph by Avi Klapfer

NEW DROPOFF

*There once was an old woman
who kept a turtle and a megapode, the incubator bird,
as pets. One day while she was away in the taro field, the
animals made a nest in the hot ashes of her cooking fire
so that the heat might incubate their eggs. When the woman
returned and found the mess, she angrily chased the animals
out of the house forever. Saddened by their fate, the turtle
crawled into the sea with the megapode on its back, and
slowly swam toward the Rock Islands. And so today in Belau,
the turtle must lay its eggs on the beach, where they incubate
in the heat of the sand; and the megapode must lay its
eggs in the forest, where they incubate in the heat of the soil.*

New Dropoff is located along a large, rounded corner of Palau's
southwestern barrier reef. This is another spectacular dropoff where you are
likely to encounter everything from nudibranchs to grey reef sharks. The reef
begins at twenty feet and slopes steeply to a shelf at 250 feet before plummeting
to the 1,000-foot bottom. The vertical face is cut with canyons and deep crevices,
providing a dramatic backdrop for a variety of marine life. Be aware that the
currents along this reef can be tricky, pushing you down into deeper water at
times. If you dive this area when the current is strong, watch your depth.

Hard and soft corals thrive along this dropoff and are home to colorful
nudibranchs and tiny, transparent shrimps. Decorator crabs, covered by the

*As if dusted by the morning frost, this unusual variety of black coral blooms white. This
particular deep-water species is generally found at depths greater than one hundred feet. Only
the skeleton of black coral is actually black. When alive, the animal varies in color from yellow,
orange, brown to white. Black coral has become a popular material for making jewelry in many
tropical areas and has been harvested extensively. There has been little commercial interest in
the black coral in Palau, and it is still found on many of the reefs.* Photograph by Avi Klapfer

sponges and small corals they attach to their shells for camouflage, scurry along the limestone rocks, while clownfish dive among the flowing tentacles of their host anemone. The nutrient-rich water of the incoming tide attracts schools of barracuda, jacks, and fusiliers. Grey reef and blacktip reef sharks are often seen and occasionally a hawksbill turtle glides by in the distance.

A large, rare variety of black coral with white polyps grows along this dropoff, its silver tentacles contrasting sharply with its dark skeleton. Sea fans covered with crinoids gently sway in the current, and exotic tropical fish feed among the rich variety of corals.

As beautiful as it is harmful, a graceful jellyfish drifts along the reef. Its long, flowing tentacles are armed with nematocysts, microscopic harpoons that inject toxin into its prey.
Photograph by Avi Klapfer

NGEMELIS DROPOFF

*L*ong ago in the soft light
of the new moon, two lovers met on a secluded beach on the
island of Ngemelis. When they awoke in the morning,
there was a nest of turtle eggs near the spot where
they had been sleeping, and the girl's grass skirt was gone.
While she was making another skirt from the fronds of the palm
tree, the lovers agreed to meet again fifteen days later on
the night of the full moon. They arrived on the appointed
evening, and as they lay by the beach they saw a
turtle crawling toward them with fragments of the
young girl's lost skirt entangled in its flipper. And this was
how it was discovered that the egg-laying cycle of the turtle
corresponds to the phases of the moon.

The great wall at Ngemelis (pronounced NEM-e-lis) is one of the most famous dropoffs in the world. The reef begins in a mere five feet of water yet falls off in a sheer vertical drop of over 800 feet. Nicknamed "Big Drop" by the locals, this spectacular wall is covered with such lush growth of marine life that it is as popular for snorkeling as it is for diving.

Ngemelis Dropoff begins just west of German Channel, the shallow pass that cuts through Palau's southwestern barrier reef. Isolated beaches fringe the shores of many of the islands in this area, some of which are used as nesting grounds by hawksbill turtles. The season that hawksbills nest in Palau extends roughly from June to January, when females crawl up the beach to lay their eggs in nests they dig in the sand. Turtles lay eggs several times during the season on a fifteen-day cycle, generally returning to the same beach on the nights

Ngemelis Dropoff is famous for its sheer vertical wall that drops more than 800 feet yet begins just five feet from the water's surface. Photograph by Rick Tegeler

of a new and full moon.

One of the more beautiful times to dive the Big Drop is in the morning, when the sun shines straight on this east-facing wall, highlighting the intense colors. Wine-red sea fans, purple soft corals, and velvet-green tree corals grow in as little as twenty feet of water, making the shallow areas a favorite with photographers as well as snorkelers. Clownfish, anemones, and brightly colored Indo-Pacific clams nestle among the golden fields of leather coral that cover the top of the reef. Giant bushes of black coral and sea fans of every variety adorn the vertical face of the wall. Grey reef sharks cruise the deeper areas of the dropoff, but it is not uncommon to see some of the more curious in water as shallow as ten feet.

Along the northernmost section of this dropoff, there is a small cut in the top of the reef where dive boats often anchor at the beginning of the dive. Just north of this area, a sea fan that measures eighteen feet from top to bottom is growing in ninety feet of water. This is the largest known sea fan in Palau.

A little farther north of the sea fan, a massive anchor ball and chain hangs from the wall in forty feet of water. This chain once stretched from east to west across the entire bay. During World War II, this area was used as a deep-water anchorage by the U.S. military. The navy installed the chain to secure floating pontoon docks that stored supplies. The supplies were off-loaded from the larger ships, then transferred to the troops stationed at Peleliu Island. When U.S. troops pulled out of Palau, the chain was simply cut in half, one piece falling to either side of the bay. Today it is a haunting reminder of a more violent time in Palau's history.

Palau is famous for its enormous sea fans, but rarely do they grow this large—eighteen feet from top to bottom. Unlike many other corals, sea fans are less dependent on light for growth. Often the largest members of this species are found at depths between eighty and 110 feet, where they are less likely to be damaged or broken by the great storm waves that occur during typhoons. Photograph by Mitchell P. Warner

GERMAN CHANNEL

At one time in Belau, men fished the lagoon with a huge net made from coconut fronds. Once the fish were cornered, they were carefully driven into the osel, a small circular trap within the net where they could be easily speared. This difficult task required the efforts of many men, and if mistakes were made insults would fly, regardless of rank or position. Insults sometimes involved another's mother—the ultimate offense in this matrilineal culture. Although swearing in this manner is not proper, etiquette on land and on sea differs according to need. Insults among men involved in any strenuous work are excused as tekoi el kereker, "words of the lagoon."

German Channel is a long, shallow cut through the southwestern barrier reef that leads from Palau's protected inner lagoon to the open ocean. The channel was made by the Germans at the turn of the century so that ships carrying phosphate mined from the southern island of Angaur could have safe passage to Koror. Today it is used almost daily by dive boats on their way to the popular dive sites in southern Palau, and it is still the only pass through the southwestern barrier reef. Depth of the channel varies with the tide but averages a mere ten feet. As dive boats approach the shallow reef, the blue ocean water turns into rich shades of turquoise and aquamarine that melt into the distant horizon of the cloud-filled sky.

Manta rays, Manta alfredi, are plankton eaters and often feed in German Channel on a changing tide. Mantas are seen throughout the year around the outer barrier reefs of Palau. During their mating season from July to August, groups of twenty or more individuals can often be found. Mantas in the open ocean can grow to twenty feet and weigh nearly a ton, but the mantas generally found near the reef have a wing span of only six or seven feet. Photograph by Ed Robinson

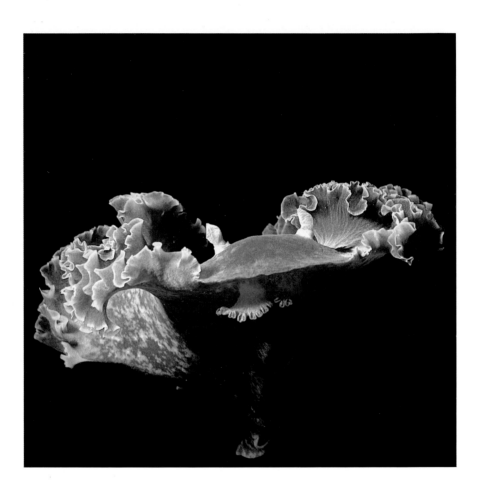

Manta rays frequently feed in this shallow channel on a changing tide, hanging motionless in the current as plankton-rich water sweeps into their open mouths. If a manta is sighted, dive boats often stop to let divers snorkel with these magnificent creatures. Mantas, unlike stingrays, have no poisonous spines at the base of their tails, so they are not dangerous to divers. Unfortunately, they are very wary and will usually flee at the first sight of divers in the water.

German Channel is not dived often because the visibility here is rarely as good as at the dropoffs along the outer barrier reef. But boats occasionally stop at the mouth of the channel where the sixty-foot bottom is scattered with large coral heads and small patch reefs. The sweeping sand areas between the coral are home to stingrays and the occasional nurse shark, and also to garden eels, extremely shy animals that live in small tubes in the sand. Often you will see groups of a hundred or more of these eels rising out of their holes and rhythmically swaying in unison with the passing current. They quickly retreat, however, at the slightest hint of approaching divers.

With wings of flowing velvet, the Spanish dancer, Hexabranchus sanguineus, swims along the reef. This spectacular nudibranch generally crawls along the bottom in search of food, but when disturbed it swims with wavelike undulations of its mantle. This nocturnal creature, which can grow to twelve inches, is rarely seen during the day. Its deep red body and brilliant orange gills make it a prized photographic subject. Photograph by Jeff La Douce

TURTLE COVE

*Long ago on the island of
Ngercheu, there lived a woman whose daughter was about
to give birth. But before the baby was born, the old
woman died, and her soul passed to the place on the island of
Angaur where all spirits stop before they go on. The old
woman asked the others at this place if she could return to
care for her daughter, for in those days women in labor
often died. The spirits agreed, but warned the old woman
that once she left them she could never return. So the
old woman went back to the island of Ngercheu, and her
daughter soon gave birth to a beautiful child. And that
child had children and those children had children. To this
day, the spirit of the old woman wanders the island and
protects her clan and their land from all harm.*

Turtle Cove is located south of German Channel, just across
the bay from Ngemelis Dropoff and several hundred yards off a sandy beach
that was once used by turtles to lay their eggs.

The dive begins by drifting through an oval-shaped hole in the top of a
shallow reef that is generally covered with five to ten feet of water, depending
on the tide. A descent into the hole brings you to two exits that open onto a
vertical wall, one at twenty-five feet and another at fifty feet. Golden sea fans,
as delicate as lace, frame the exit at fifty feet, and Moorish idols feed among
the orange tube corals and chrome-yellow encrusting sponges. Schools of
graceful pyramid butterflyfish greet you as you swim from the hole onto the
dropoff, while blue and gold fusiliers glide by in the distance. Bottom-dwelling

*Rivaling the beauty of any flower, the delicate tentacles of a tube coral, Tubastrea sp.,
are usually seen only at night. They often expand during the day, however, in the relative darkness of the overhanging ledges at Turtle Cove.* Photograph by Al Giddings

leopard sharks sometimes sleep in the sandy area just below this exit, but they are most often found in the deeper water between one hundred and 130 feet.

Once out onto the dropoff, divers usually swim to the right along a vertical wall that is honeycombed with holes where nocturnal squirrelfish, soldierfish, and bright orange bigeyes hover in the shadows. In Palau the barred squirrelfish, *Adioryx diadema,* is known as *techelabilis,* which means "meat of the dog." Palauans don't eat dogs. Apparently they don't think much of the barred squirrelfish either.

The top of the reef grows to within fifteen feet of the surface so you can dive any depth you choose. Lush soft corals, exquisite sea fans, and leather corals with delicate, daisylike polyps adorn the vertical face of the wall. At night this dropoff is covered with lionfish that by day usually hide deep within the crevices of the reef. The resident school of black snapper—mottled black and brown fish with big golden eyes—generally appears at some point during the dive, and grey reef sharks often cruise the blue open water just within the limits of visibility.

A prized photographic subject, the clown triggerfish, Balistoides conspicillum, is often seen along the top of the reef at Turtle Cove. Photograph by Rick Tegeler

*There once was a fisherman
who went hunting for turtles. While he was paddling his
canoe, he noticed a large hawksbill—a turtle prized
for its shell, from which special Belauan money was made.
Without pausing to anchor his canoe, he dove into the
water. After a great deal of struggle, he surfaced with the
turtle. But by this time his canoe had drifted far away.
As he swam toward the canoe with the turtle in his arms,
the canoe drifted farther and farther away. Finally he let go
of the turtle, but he was so exhausted and his canoe was
so far away that the humiliated fisherman had to swim back
to his village without the turtle or his canoe. Those who try
to do two jobs at once often accomplish neither.*

Ngedebus (pronounced Ned-e-BOOS) Dropoff is located south of Turtle Cove along a stretch of reef that is covered with small plate corals and large sea fans. The reef grows to within twenty feet of the surface, drops vertically in some places, gradually slopes in others, and is dramatically cut with canyons and deep crevices. There is a small peninsula that juts out into open ocean along one section of the reef. Depending on the direction of the current, dives either begin north of this point or south and drift toward the corner.

As the name implies, hawksbill turtles, <u>Eretmochelys imbricata</u>, have a projecting hawk-like upper jaw. Barnacles often attach to the shells of older turtles as can be seen in the photograph. Historically, hawksbills have played a significant role in Palauan culture. Their eggs have long been considered a delicacy, and their shells were molded into money plates and used as "women's money." Hawksbills are listed as an endangered species worldwide; they are still common in Palau, but their numbers and average size have decreased in recent years. Local laws restrict the size of turtles that can be taken and the size and number of eggs that can be removed from nests, but these laws are difficult to enforce due to limited resources. Photograph by George Balazs

Hawksbill turtles are occasionally seen in this area. They generally sleep in the afternoon, so they are more often seen in the morning swimming openly on the reef. From midday to late afternoon, you can sometimes find them sleeping in crevices or in caves in the reef. Turtles breathe air but can stay submerged for several hours when they sleep. When awake, they must surface for air every ten to thirty minutes. However, when they are frightened—for example, if grabbed by divers—they must surface more often. Hawksbills are an endangered species. Divers should appreciate the rare opportunity to see these turtles in the wild and not bother them in any way.

Bottom-dwelling sharks are also found along this reef, wedged into the crevices or under the sandy ledges between eighty and one hundred feet. There are two types of bottom-dwelling sharks in Palau—the nurse shark, *Nebrius concolor*, a genus common in oceans around the world; and the leopard shark, *Stegostoma varium*, which is unique to the Indo-Pacific. These sharks are similar in appearance, with broad, rounded heads and long tails that tilt slightly upward. Leopard sharks can be easily identified by the small brown spots covering their yellowish body; the nurse shark has a smooth gray coloration. Nurse sharks can grow to an impressive eleven feet, leopard sharks to eight feet, but their tails make up almost half their lengths. Both sharks feed on molluscs and small crustaceans and are relatively harmless to divers. They are sluggish swimmers and will often let divers approach them, but divers who have harassed these normally docile creatures have been bitten.

The leopard shark, <u>Stegostoma varium</u>, is native only to the Indo-Pacific. These bottom-dwelling sharks are occasionally seen along Ngedebus Dropoff wedged into crevices or under sandy ledges. Photograph by Avi Klapfer

In the most distant past, there was a demigod from Peleliu Island who kept a school of mullet fish as his pets. And from the eastern coast of the island of Babeldaob, there was a demigod who kept the strong current of the sea as his pet. At that time in Belau, the demigods traveled around the islands, visiting one another and seeing to it that human beings maintained their good behavior. On one visit the two demigods decided to exchange pets. So today in Belau, a large school of mullet fish appears in the Ngiwal Lagoon off the eastern coast of Babeldaob during their spawning season, and strong currents and big waves are often found on the southern side of Peleliu Island.

When diving the south wall at Peleliu (pronounced PEL-a-loo) Island, you are on the southernmost tip of the barrier reef that surrounds Palau. On one side of you is the Philippine Sea, on the other, the great Pacific. This is wild, open ocean, and the marine life is spectacular.

A shallow shelf extends from the southern shore of the island and abruptly drops 400 feet. Immense gorgonian sea fans cascade down the vertical wall. Black wire corals coiled like bedsprings are covered with neon yellow polyps that feed in the current. Basketball-sized crinoids cling to sea fans and wire corals for the best possible position in the nutrient-rich water. Huge stands of black coral trees are found as shallow as fifty feet.

This wall is covered with marine life, but it is the pelagic fish that command most of the attention. According to local fishermen, the underwater point just off the southern tip of the island is one of the best-known spawning grounds

---

Grey reef sharks, Carcharhinus amblyrhynchos, are a common sight along the Peleliu wall. Photograph by Rick Tegeler

for many of the reef fish found in Palau. The abundance of this fish larvae attracts hordes of predators, including jacks, barracuda, and grey reef sharks. During April and May, skip jacks spawn in this area, and schools of fish numbering in the thousands cloud the water with flashes of silver and gray.

Palauan fishermen have long known that this area is an excellent fishing ground. A tragic incident during World War II graphically illustrated the reason for the abundance of fish. In September 1944 American troops invaded the beach on the southeastern side of this heavily fortified island, then held by the Japanese. Much blood was spilled. Instead of dispersing, the blood-red water moved all the way around the southern tip of the island, where a circling current confined it within a stationary pool that was visible for days. This same current confines the pelagic fish larvae to the spawning grounds, attracting hundreds of feeding fish.

The most popular areas to dive are located on the southern side of the island, but there are areas along the eastern coast that have not yet been fully explored and might hold some exciting surprises. However, the diving at Peleliu is completely dependent upon the weather. The water is often rough, and currents can be strong enough to make conditions too dangerous for diving. Trips to the area are not offered regularly, and Peleliu is recommended for experienced divers only.

After a morning dive at Peleliu, a fascinating tour of the island can be arranged and is well worth the extra expense. One of the most intense battles of the Pacific war was waged here in September of 1944. In fighting that lasted nearly three months, an estimated 11,000 Japanese and 1,000 Americans lost their lives. The Japanese had turned the island's many natural caves into nearly impregnable fortresses by constructing walls of reinforced concrete to protect the entrances. Some of the larger caves were even equipped with electric lighting, ventilating systems, and radio communications. Today tanks, machine guns, and other heavy artillery are scattered throughout the island—their rusting remains now slowly being reclaimed by the jungle.

A fragile crinoid, no larger than a thumbnail, hides among the delicate branches of a soft coral, Dendronephthya sp. Photograph by Rick Tegeler

ANGAUR

*O*n the southwestern shore
*of the island of Angaur, there is a place known as Ngedloch
Beach, where the souls of the dead stop before passing on
to the other side. One day a man was gathering pandanus
leaves near this sacred place and came upon a group of spirits
holding a feast. The spirits, surprised at being discovered,
gave the man a beautifully carved wooden bowl filled with
taro as a gift for the people of his village. But while he was
on his way home, the spirits took away the taro and broke the
wooden bowl so humans would not see how well the souls
lived and would continue to prefer life to death.*

Angaur (pronounced ANG-our) is the southernmost island of the main Palau archipelago, approximately one and a half hours from Koror by boat. Because the island is located outside the barrier reef, dive operators will make the trip only when the weather is calm. There are daily airline flights to Angaur, but to date there are no scuba shops on the island. If you want to dive these pristine reefs, you will have to make special arrangements with the dive operators in Koror.

Angaur offers experienced divers a chance to explore reefs that are rarely dived. Because the island is surrounded by open ocean, schools of barracuda, jacks, and other large pelagics are common. Hammerhead sharks occasionally appear along the reef as well as oceanic white tip sharks, a very aggressive open-ocean predator. Angaur fishermen report that they routinely catch 200-pound dog-tooth tuna just off the reef, and several times a year harmless plankton-

Magnificent and awe-inspiring yet unpredictable and dangerous, oceanic white tip sharks, Carcharhinus longimanus, *have been seen by divers around the reefs of Angaur. Striped pilot fish often swim with these large open-ocean predators.* Photograph by Al Giddings

eating whale sharks, which can grow to sixty feet, are spotted within a few hundred yards of the western shores.

Local fishermen report a sunken ship, possibly from World War II, on the eastern side of the island, and there are rumors of a Spanish galleon lying in just one hundred feet of water off the southeastern shore. But divers have yet to find either ship.

The most popular areas to dive are found along the southern and western sides of the island. The northern and eastern shores are rarely explored because of the heavy surf. The reefs vary from steeply sloping walls to those with slow, gradual slopes and generally begin in twenty to fifty feet of water. The tops of most reefs are barren, possibly due to strong waves that hit these areas, but once you get past forty or fifty feet the corals begin to flourish and the reefs bloom with giant sea fans. The huge undercuts in the deeper areas are thick with black coral, and large caves beckon from the darker recesses of the dropoffs.

Many refer to Angaur as the Palauan Outback, and with a tour around the island it is easy to see why. There is a rugged, easygoing charm to the 214 residents, whose main occupation is fishing. The powerful waves crashing against the rocky northern coastline contrast sharply with the peaceful waters of the pristine southern beaches. Dramatic blowholes are found along the northern coast, as well as a pack of wild monkeys—descendants of ones brought during the German occupation to test the toxicity of the air in the phosphate mines.

Angaur, like Peleliu, boasts its own share of World War II relics. The island was the site of a large U.S. airbase during the war, and several crash-landed aircraft—large B-24 bombers and a nearly intact F-4 Corsair fighter—lie adjacent to one of the abandoned runways in the dense jungle along the northeastern coast.

The remains of this nearly intact Corsair fighter plane lie in the dense jungle along Angaur's northeastern coast, among towering trees whose fascinating root structure adds a surreal feeling to the scene.

CORAL GARDENS

There once was a fisherman who set his traps in an area of the reef that was unfamiliar to him. In order to find his traps, he had to triangulate their locations. But instead of marking the new locations from land, he used the clouds, and the foolish man never found his fish traps again.

There are actually three dive sites known as Coral Gardens, all of which have in common beautiful hard coral formations. The original Coral Gardens is located on the northeast side of Ngerchong Island, a small island east of German Channel. Here the forty-foot bottom is scattered with large mounds of brain and star coral. On the southern side of the island, there is an another area known as Coral Gardens where large table corals are the dominant species. Yet another area, Ngemelis Coral Gardens, is just north of New Dropoff. Here the shallow reef gently slopes to great depths and is covered with a variety of species, each growing in its own distinctive shape, from mounds of brain coral to flat plate corals to fields of branching staghorn.

Palau is one of the few areas of the world with such a rich diversity of coral. Scientists estimate that there are more than 700 species. Although soft corals and sea fans usually get most of the attention, the intricate patterns, subtle colors, and varied shapes of hard corals have a special beauty all their own.

Hard or "stony" corals are the true builders of the reef. Surprisingly, coral reef structures hundreds of feet high and millions of years old are the work of one of the smallest and simplest members of the animal kingdom.

The Coral Gardens dive sites are known for their beautiful hard coral formations.
Photograph by Ed Robinson

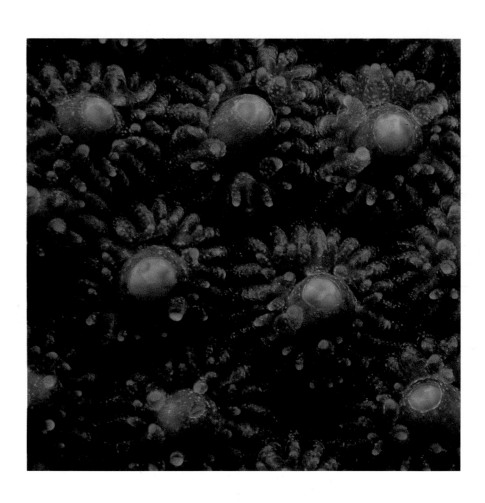

An individual coral animal, or polyp, is nothing more than a fleshy sack topped by a mouth ringed with tentacles. Each polyp extracts calcium and carbonate ions from sea water and deposits them around itself in a close-fitting cup of solid limestone. The polyp secretes this external skeleton throughout its lifetime, thereby increasing the height and thickness of its surrounding walls. Given adequate food, sunlight, and other environmental conditions, the polyp reproduces by splitting into two polyps, then four, and so on until the individual has formed a colony. Coral also reproduces by spawning—releasing eggs and sperm into the surrounding water, producing a planktonic larva that eventually undergoes metamorphosis and settles onto the reef to begin a new coral colony.

Only the thin surface layer of coral is alive. Underlying the living exterior are the skeletons of billions of plants and animals that have cemented together, forming the reef structure. Living within the thin surface layer of the coral's tissues are minute, single-celled algae called zooxanthellae (pronounced zo-zan-THEL-ee), which provide nutrients for the coral and give it much of its color. Without these zooxanthellae, most coral would appear white.

Many hard corals are nocturnal and extend their fleshy tentacles only at night, which changes their appearance dramatically. During the day the polyps are withdrawn into their limestone skeletons, but a thin layer of the animal's flesh covers the entire coral colony at all times. Kicking, sitting, or standing on a coral colony can tear this tissue. Torn tissue can become infected with an algae that can kill the surrounding area and spread like a cancer. Although coral is amazingly resilient, severe or repeated injury can eventually lead to the death of an entire coral colony.

Coral reproduces in several ways, one of which is by spawning—releasing eggs and sperm into the surrounding water. The orange balls in the photograph are egg cases containing both eggs and sperm, which eventually produce a planktonic larva that setles onto the reef to begin a new coral colony. Photograph by Mitchell P. Warner

JELLYFISH LAKE

*R*alm taoch—
"Like estuary water, neither salt nor fresh."
Estuary water is composed of both saltwater and
fresh rainwater, and is therefore neither. Palauans apply
this saying to a person who is indecisive.

It doesn't get much stranger than this—millions of harmless
jellyfish silently pulsing around you, sliding between your fins, bumping into
your mask. These caramel-colored, softball-sized jellyfish, with stings too weak
for all but the most sensitive person to feel, live in Jellyfish Lake, a landlocked
saltwater lake in Palau.

The jellyfish in the lake are members of the genus *Mastigias*, a jellyfish
commonly found in the Palau Lagoon whose powerful stinging tentacles are
used for protection and for capturing planktonic prey. It is believed that ances-
tors of these *Mastigias* jellyfish became trapped in the lake millions of years
ago when volcanic forces uplifted Palau's submerged reefs, transforming deep
pockets in the reefs into landlocked saltwater lakes. Because there was little
food and few predators in the lake, their long, clublike tentacles gradually
evolved into stubby appendages unable to sting, and the jellyfish came to rely
on the symbiotic algae living within their tissues for nutrients. The algae capture energy from the sun and transform it into food for the jellyfish. In turn,
the jellyfish swim near the surface during the day to ensure that the algae
receive enough sunlight for photosynthesis to occur, which nourishes the

*Of the more than thirty saltwater lakes in Palau, Jellyfish Lake is one of the most
unusual. Here, a jellyfish trapped in the lake millions of years ago has evolved into a nonstinging
form not known to exist anywhere else in the world. Scientists estimate the school of jellyfish
to be over 1.6 million.*

algae. Every morning the school of jellyfish, estimated at more than 1.6 million, migrates across the lake to the opposite shore, each jellyfish rotating counterclockwise so that the algae on all sides of its bell receive equal sunlight. In the afternoon the jellyfish turn and swim back across the lake. At night they descend to the lake's middle layer, where they absorb the nitrogen that fertilizes their algae.

Although the *Mastigias* jellyfish is the dominant species, the lake is also home to the disk-shaped, transparent moon jellyfish, *Aurelia aurita,* whose stings are also too weak to feel. Three species of small fish and an anemone that grows near the shore are the only other creatures known to live in this unusual underwater environment.

Jellyfish Lake is located in the interior of Eil Malk Island, a large, uninhabited rock island about thirty minutes from Koror by boat. Once you reach the island, getting to the lake requires a fifteen-minute hike over a one-hundred-foot jungled ridge. The trail is littered with sharp limestone and slippery, decaying leaves, so rubber-soled shoes or diving booties are advised. There are several tall poisonous trees near the beginning of the trail whose trunks ooze an obvious black, sticky sap that blisters skin, similar to a rash caused by poison oak, so watch where you put your hands.

The jellyfish swim near the surface during the day, so all you need to bring is your snorkeling gear. If you feel like lugging your scuba equipment over the ridge, be aware that even though the upper half of the lake is a harmless mix of saltwater and fresh rainwater, at fifty feet there is a bacterial layer of deoxygenated water laced with highly toxic concentrations of hydrogen sulfide. Although the concentration in the lake is not lethal, it can cause severe long-term respiratory problems. If you dive at all, do not dive below fifty feet.

Once you reach the lake, the search for the elusive school of jellyfish begins with a snorkel through a small mangrove-lined swamp whose depth and visibility is only three feet. The shallow channel is an obstacle course of submerged rocks, and the silt bottom is easily stirred up by kicking fins so be considerate of the person behind you. The school of jellyfish moves throughout the day, and finding them often requires a swim of several hundred yards through a hazy mixture of saltwater and fresh rainwater where visibility is only fifteen feet. As you search the water for signs of life, an eerie silence permeates the air, broken only by the occasional sounds of birds overhead.

Just as you begin to wonder what you're doing in this jungle-enclosed lake, a jellyfish often pulses into view. Then another...and another. Soon you are surrounded by a cloud of golden *medusae*. As you swim among these fragile creatures, use as little movement as possible—even a gentle kick with your fins can send them somersaulting through the water, and their delicate tissues are easily torn. Sadly, some divers throw the jellyfish around like softballs or remove them from the lake and dump them in the outer lagoon, where they have no chance of survival. This unique form of jellyfish is not known to exist anywhere else in the world, and its private universe has remained untouched for thousands of years. It would be tragic to see its numbers diminished by man's curiosity and ignorance.

GIANT CLAM GARDEN

*G*iant clams are becoming a rare sight in the Indo-Pacific, largely due to the massive commercial exploitation by foreign poachers. Palau has escaped the devastation of this illegal poaching, and giant tridacna clams are still found on many reefs. Near one of Palau's rock islands, there are dozens of these giants living in just ten to thirty feet of water. Boats often stop in this area after a day of diving on the outer barrier reef so that divers can snorkel with these colossal creatures, the largest bivalve mollusc in the world.

Not all clams are giants, however. There are seven species in the *Tridacnid* family, from the small *Tridacna crocea* with its brightly colored mantle to the enormous *T. gigas*, which grows up to four feet in length and weighs as much as 600 pounds. All clams are thought to live for decades. The grand old giants may be more than half a century old.

Clams receive most of their nutrients from symbiotic algae that grow within their tissues, so they must live in shallow, sunlit areas of the reef. The smaller species bore into coral so that only their mantles are exposed, while the larger clams lie on the open, sandy bottom of the reef.

The larger clams have thick, fleshy mantles that prevent them from closing their shells completely, so contrary to wild stories of giant killer clams, it is next to impossible to get your hand or foot stuck inside the shell.

Near Hokkens Island a garden of giant clams lives in just ten to thirty feet of water. Giant tridacna clams can grow up to four feet in length and weigh nearly 600 pounds. Clams have been an important source of protein for people in the Indo-Pacific for centuries. They have survived years of subsistence fishing, but today they are becoming a rare sight in many areas due to illegal poaching by foreign fishermen. Photograph by Mitchell P. Warner

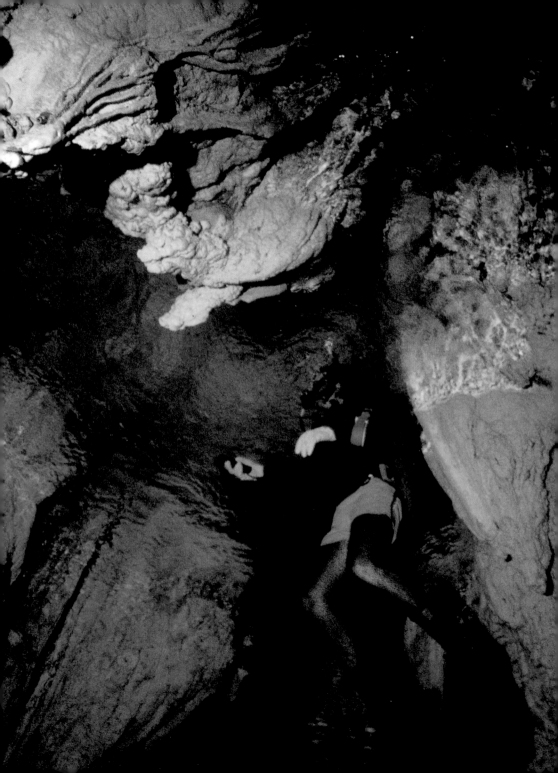

CHANDELIER CAVE

There once was a spear fisherman from Koror who went searching for food near the island of Ngarol. Using goggles of wood with lenses of tortoiseshell polished to a transparent thinness, he floated quietly on the surface until he saw an enormous grouper, the largest fish he had ever seen. He aimed his spear and shot, striking the grouper but not killing it. The angry fish lunged into the darkness of a nearby cave, towing the determined fisherman behind. The fisherman held his breath for as long as he could, but finally he realized that the grouper had won. Nearly unconscious and desperate for air, he released the spear and swam upward into the darkness. Suddenly his head burst into a pocket of air in the ceiling of the cave and the fisherman lived to tell the story of Yii Temekai, the "Cave of the Grouper."

———————— ✺ ————————

Chandelier Cave was once an air-filled cavern, possibly formed during the last Ice Age, millions of years ago when the ocean was one hundred feet shallower. Today it is a fascinating underwater cave dripping with ancient columns of stalactites and stalagmites. Palauans know the cave as *Yii Temekai*, the Cave of the Grouper, because of the legendary tale of the heroic fisherman. Divers nicknamed it Chandelier Cave because of the beautiful mineral deposits that sparkle like chandeliers on the dry ceilings of the cave.

The cave is located in the uninhabited island of Ngarol, just minutes from Koror by boat. It is a series of four chambers, each deeper into the island's interior than the next, with ceilings that rise above the water level. This can be a place of intense fascination or your worst nightmare, depending

A diver examines underwater stalactites in Chandelier Cave. Photograph by Rick Tegeler on how you feel about cave diving. It is a thrilling experience for most, but those who are the least bit claustrophobic should think twice before entering. And no one should explore this cave without a knowledgeable guide.

The entrance to the cave is through a large hole that cuts into the limestone footing of the island, fifteen feet below the water's surface. Before entering, adjust your buoyancy so as not to disturb the soft silt bottom of the cave's entrance. This sandy bottom slopes to a depth of sixty feet as you begin your ascent toward the first air-pocket in the ceiling of the cave. Dark, ominous shapes of ancient stalactites, their tips now partially submerged, begin to appear in your dive light as you swim through an upper layer of fresh water that has filtered through hundreds of feet of island overhead. It was through this process that the stalactites were formed centuries ago when the cave was dry. As fresh rainwater slowly seeped through the rotting vegetation of the island, it formed humic acid that dissolved the limestone rock and carried it along until it reached the ceiling of the cave. Once there, the dripping water slowly evaporated over time, redepositing its load of calcium rock in the shape of dripstone columns.

Today much of this water falls into the cavern below, forming a lens of crystal-clear fresh water that floats on top of the dense saltwater base. Stalactites are still being formed in the air-filled chambers on the ceiling of the cave. In the first chamber, these mineral deposits have taken the shape of a chandelier, giving the cave its name. Fresh air also filters through the porous limestone, providing safe, breathable air inside the cavern.

As you swim deeper into the island's interior, senses can become disoriented in such strange, unfamiliar surroundings. Even with dive lights, it is sometimes difficult to tell if you are ascending or descending when exploring the rear chambers. The upper layer of fresh water is so clear that it feels as if you are swimming through air, further confusing your senses.

In the final chamber, the floor of the cave rises sharply so that you can stand head and shoulders out of the water. If you remove your dive gear you can then crawl through a narrow passageway leading to a completely dry chamber, which in turn winds hundreds of more feet through the island. Frozen waterfalls of sparkling mineral deposits flow from the walls, and stalactites glisten like icicles from the dry ceiling of the cave. Strange crystal-clear formations called helectites grow from the walls and ceilings in every direction, and seem to defy gravity with their unusual twists and turns. This mystical, enchanting place is a world unto itself, a fantasyland whose wonders few people ever see.

The rear, dry chambers of Chandelier Cave are a fantasyland of mineral deposits that sparkle like diamonds in the glow of a dive light. Along with stalactites, unusual formations known as helectites are found on the floor, walls, and ceiling of the cave. These pencil-thin, crystal-clear formations grow in every direction, defying gravity with their unusual twists and turns. Photograph by Mitchell P. Warner

LIGHTHOUSE CHANNEL

*There once was a woman
whose husband was turned into a nut tree by an evil spirit.
Not long after this, the woman gave birth to a baby girl.
As the girl grew up, the mother told her daughter never to
eat the nuts from the nearby tree. One day while her
mother was away, the girl picked a handful of nuts. The
mother suddenly appeared, and the daughter, in her shame,
hid the nuts in her mouth and ran into the sea. Once in
the water she turned into a dugong, a sea cow, and
disappeared. And so today one can see a bulging in the
jaws of the dugong that had once been the nuts in the
girl's mouth. When a dugong is caught, it breathes like a
human, and when it is about to be killed, the tears
of the crying daughter can be seen flowing from its eyes.*

Lighthouse Channel (also known as Malakal Passage) is the
main entrance to Malakal Harbor from the eastern side of Palau. Its Palauan
name, *Kesebekuu,* which means moray eel, is far more descriptive, for this
natural channel gently winds through the reef like a graceful moray. At sunset
dugongs often come from deeper water to feed in the shallow sea grass beds
on both sides of the channel. Dugongs are extremely shy and difficult to
approach, so divers rarely see these unusual, endangered mammals. At one
time the dugong was hunted for its delicious meat, but this delicacy was allowed
only to Palauans of the highest rank, thereby creating a form of controlled
harvesting that protected them from overhunting. Royal bracelets were made

*The blue starfish, <u>Linckia laevigata</u>, is one of the many species of starfish in Palau. Unlike
other starfish, which normally emerge from under rocks or ledges only at night, this species is
often seen in the shallow areas of the reef in the daylight hours. It is believed that its deep cobalt
blue coloration protects it from the strong light of the sun.* Photograph by Ed Robinson

from the dugong vertebrae and can still be seen on the wrists of some Palauan men today. Hunting is now forbidden, but still continues illegally due to a lack of money for enforcement.

Average depth inside the channel is eighty feet, but much of the interesting marine life can be found in ten to forty feet of water. Gorgeous nudibranchs, exotic lionfish, spotted moray eels, banded coral shrimp, and starfish in flaming reds and cobalt blues are found throughout the channel. There are also numerous clownfish and their host anemones. Some of the anemones are albino, while others have brilliantly colored undersides of purple, fuchsia, or jade green. Often the anemones will close, forming spectacular balls of color.

Even the sea cucumbers are beautiful in Palau. The caramel-colored body of the leopard sea cucumber is covered with cinnamon spots circled in black. When harassed these normally lifeless creatures eject a sticky mass of spaghetti-like threads that adhere to hands like glue. Young Palauan boys used to wrap their bare feet with these threads for protection as they ran across the reef to spear fish. The sticky threads would soon mold to the foot, forming rubbery shoes that were eventually cut off after a day of spearfishing on the reef.

If you are interested in bigger animals, turtles and whitetip reef sharks occasionally swim through the channel, and spotted eagle rays sometime feed on the sandy bottom. But in order to find these animals, you have to drop down between sixty and eighty feet, where there is usually not much else to see.

Even though the larger cargo ships use the deeper channel on the western side of the islands, this is a busy area for smaller speedboats so stay to the side

---

Clownfish and anemones live together in an unusual symbiotic relationship. The tentacles of anemones are armed with microscopic harpoons called nematocysts that inject a paralyzing toxin into their prey. Although these nematocysts are harmless to humans, they are lethal to small fish and invertebrates. Clownfish are immune to these batteries of stinging capsules. The exact set of conditions needed to produce this immunity is not completely understood. It is believed that the clowning behavior of the fish — repeatedly diving into the anemone and fanning its body — transfers a chemical from the anemone to the clownfish, which in effect camouflages the fish from the stinging tentacles. Photograph by Rick Tegeler

of the channel when you surface. In addition, strong currents run through here, so count on a swift drift dive except during slack tide.

Lighthouse Channel is an exceptional shallow dive and all the more special because it was nearly destroyed in the early 1970s by the crown of thorns, a multi-armed, spine-covered starfish that feeds mainly on coral. For nearly two years, thousands of these animals ate their way across many of the reefs in Palau. A single crown of thorns is capable, by some estimates, of destroying a half-mile of reef per month. At first this plague was considered an ecological disaster, and steps were initiated to kill as many starfish as possible. Local divers began injecting the crown of thorns with formalin and gradually the number of starfish diminished.

Many scientists now believe that these periodic devastations of the reef are cyclical and liken them to beneficial forest fires. The crown of thorns favors the hardier species of coral that overgrow and kill the smaller, weaker varieties. As the stronger corals die off, the delicate, slower-growing species are given a chance for survival, thereby maintaining the diversity of the reef.

Natural phenomenon or natural disaster, whatever the reason, it took nearly ten years for the corals to recover. But Lighthouse Channel is again alive with a spectacular variety of corals and interesting marine life.

Lighthouse Channel is home to a variety of shells, from the beautiful cowry and the venomous cone to the magnificent trident trumpet. Pictured at left is the pimpled basket shell, Nassarius papillosus. Often the animal itself is as beautiful as the shell. Photograph by Avi Klapfer

SHORT DROPOFF

Long ago there were brave men in Belau who fished for sharks that fed under drifting logs off the eastern coast of the island. One day while far out to sea, a fisherman saw a shark swimming upside down near his canoe. Such unusual behavior was a warning to him that something was wrong. He began to suspect that his wife had been unfaithful so he hurried back to the village dock where the men who had not gone out fishing gathered. The angry husband, hoping to discover the guilty man, raised his spear and shouted, "I know which of you has been with my wife. Run, for your life is no longer yours." The guilty man, thinking that his identity was already known, started to run—but the foolish man had given himself away and was killed on the spot. The chief of the village praised the brave fisherman for the clever way he detected his wife's lover.

The reefs of Palau are famous for their many exotic creatures, but there are a few unusual attractions that deserve attention as well. On the eastern side of the islands, there is a large horseshoe-shaped reef known as Short Dropoff. There are several places to dive along this enormous reef, but its most unusual feature is found along the southwestern corner. Here, starting at a depth of thirty feet, hundreds of sea fans the size of beach umbrellas cascade down the sloping wall as far as you can see. These sea fans thrive in the strong current that passes here, aligning their flat, mesh network perpendicular to the

Sea fans are very efficient feeders. When their tentacles are exposed, they almost touch, enabling them to catch most of the plankton that drift through their branches. The density of a sea fan's mesh is often determined by the strength of the current where it lives. If a sea fan were taken from the quieter waters of the Turtle Cove dive site and planted at Short Dropoff, it would develop a tighter, stronger mesh to give it greater rigidity to survive its new environ-ment. Photograph by Mitchell P. Warner

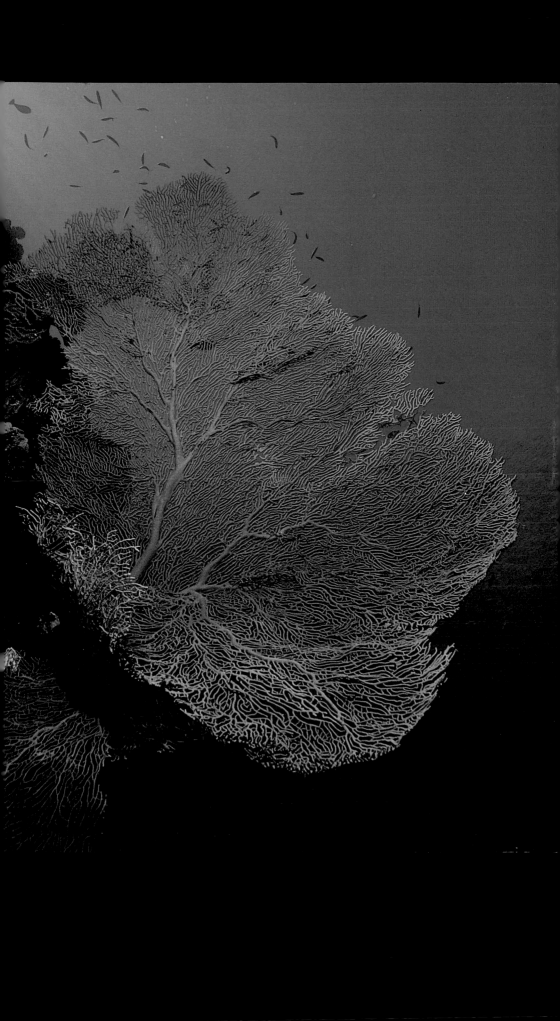

flowing water to maximize their ability to capture drifting planktonic prey. Rarely do you find such a large concentration of sea fans in one area.

Short Dropoff is located next to the Belau Trench, which at 27,000 feet is one of the deepest underwater points in the world. Because of the depth, this area was the site of extensive research on the chambered nautilus, a deep-water animal that lives between 200 and 2,000 feet. There are five known species of nautilus; one species, the *Nautilus belauensis*, was discovered in Palau in the late 1970s. Divers rarely see nautilus in the wild. Most photographs are taken of animals that have been captured in deep water and brought to shallow areas where they are released and photographed as they descend again into the depths.

During the season of northeast tradewinds (roughly October through April), the prevailing winds and currents bring drifting logs toward the eastern side of Palau. Large pelagic sharks tend to gather under drifting logs, and in ancient times this was the season for offshore shark fishing, known as *oungeuaol*. At one time shark fishing was a great event in Palau. *Oungeuaol* fishermen sailed as far as ten miles off the east coast of the islands in search of large pieces of floating driftwood. Flying fish were used as bait to bring the sharks in close to the canoes. When a shark came close enough, it was caught with a noose made of hibiscus fiber. Shark fishermen had special tattoos on their wrists. When holding out a flying fish to entice a shark through the noose, they were not to release the bait until the shark's snout touched the tattoo. There was great danger involved in catching a shark, and *oungeuaol* fishermen were highly regarded members of their village.

As elusive as the mythical "ship of pearl" alluded to by poet Oliver Wendell Holmes, the chambered nautilus (Nautilus macromphalus pictured here) is rarely seen by divers. These exquisite animals, whose shell is lined with mother-of-pearl, live at depths between 200 and 2,000 feet. As one scientist explains, "If you happen to see a nautilus in the wild, you're diving too deep." Photograph by Avi Klapfer

KAYANGEL

*There once was a man
who wanted to punish his wife, so he set her adrift to sea on
a bamboo raft. But the gods had warned the woman of
her angry husband's plot and told her to gather a branch of
the hibiscus tree and fill half a coconut shell with ashes.
Days later when the woman had drifted far outside the reef,
she scattered the ashes over the ocean as the gods had
instructed. She then stuck the hibiscus branch to the bottom
of the sea and covered the top half with the coconut shell.
Her actions formed an island, and the woman was saved.
The island is now known as Kayangel, and the hibiscus
tree, a sacred one, still grows.*

Kayangel (pronounced Kaw-AN-gle), the northernmost group
of islands in Palau, is one of the most beautiful places on earth. Its four palm-covered islands, circled by white sand beaches, fringe a transparent, turquoise lagoon, forming a picture-perfect coral atoll. Only one of the islands is inhabited. There are no cars, no electricity, and only 110 people. Life in the village is peaceful and reminiscent of Palauan days of old.

Kayangel is two and a half hours from Koror by boat. So few divers come here that the dive sites are unnamed. The reefs vary from gently sloping coral gardens on the eastern side of the island to steeply sloping dropoffs near Ulach Pass, the main channel on the western side. Turtles, leopard sharks, and spotted eagle rays are often seen around this pass, and a number of giant clams live along the reef. There are good areas to snorkel in the thirty-foot-deep lagoon, and exotic sea shells lie scattered about the deserted beaches.

Some divers feel that the vertical dropoffs and schools of pelagic fish in the Ngemelis area of southern Palau are far more dramatic, but Kayangel offers a different kind of appeal. Its reefs are near pristine, and the scenery above water is spectacular. There is a certain magic to this place—your footprints on one of these remote, uninhabited islands might be the first in a month. Even the sunsets are somehow more beautiful.

Ngeruangel Reef, just north of Kayangel, is even more remote. There are few places left in the world that offer such pristine reefs. Giant fields of acropora coral grow along the shallow bottom, and several ships from the Second World War, now badly blown apart from salvage attempts, lie scattered about the reefs.

Kayangel is perhaps all the more special because of the difficulty in getting there. There is no airline service to the island, boat tours to the area are not offered regularly, and the trip is expensive. In addition, the island is located outside the barrier reef so the diving is completely at the mercy of the weather. Dive operators occasionally offer a two-day trip with an overnight on one of the uninhabited islands. A one-day trip to the area can also be arranged, but boats leave Koror around 7:00 a.m. and return around 5:00 p.m. It's a long day, and there is not much time to experience the peacefulness of the islands.

Not many people see this part of Palau, but the extra time and expense it takes to get to Kayangel is well worth the effort. See it before someone builds a hotel.

Following Page: Kayangel is a classic coral atoll, the remains of an ancient volcano that sank into the ocean eons ago. The evolution of an atoll begins when a volcano erupts at the surface, forming an island. Over time corals begin to settle on the volcano's submerged slopes, creating a reef that surrounds the island. Because the volcano's foundation is unstable, it gradually sinks back into the ocean, but the reef continues to grow toward the surface. With earth movements and sea level fluctuations, the reef becomes exposed to the air and vegetation forms. Today the four islands of Kayangel sit atop the rim of a submerged volcano. Photograph by Avi Klapfer

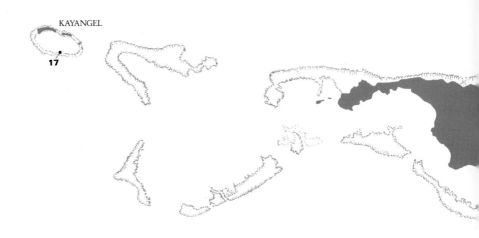

KAYANGEL

17

P H I L I P P I N E

S E A

DIVE SITES

N ←

P A C I F I C

O C E A N

BABELDAOB

16

KOROR
15
14
21
NGAROL
19 **18** NGERUKTABEL
20 **13**
ROCK **12**
ISLANDS **12**

7
SEVENTY NGERCHEU
6 **8**
ULONG ISLANDS **5**
12 **9**
3 **4** PELELIU
1
10

2

ANGAUR

11

SHIPWRECKS

*I*n March of 1944, more than fifty ships of the Japanese Imperial Navy were destroyed at Palau during the American air strike Operation Desecrate. Following their devastating losses one month earlier at Truk Lagoon, the Japanese fleets relocated their main supply center and naval base to Palau. On March 30 and 31, the Americans repeated the strategy they had used so successfully in Truk—destroying major enemy bases solely with warplanes launched from the aircraft carriers of Task Force 58, under the command of Admiral Marc Mitscher.

Tipped off to the impending American attack by Japanese spotter planes, several ships of the Imperial fleet made a narrow escape through the Allied submarines that had surrounded the Palau Lagoon. The super battle-ship *Musashi*, flagship of Admiral Koga, commander of the Japanese Combined Fleet, was hit by a torpedo, but was able to limp away before the Americans mined the channels into the harbor preventing any further escape. The remaining Japanese ships were trapped in the lagoon, and after two days of intense raids they were hopelessly ablaze and sinking.

Soon after the war, many of the ships were salvaged by several professional Japanese companies as well as by a local Palauan company. Salvage operations ended in the mid-1950s, and for the next thirty years the ships were ignored.

In 1988 a book, *Desecrate l, The Shipwrecks of Palau,* by Klaus Lindemann, spurred renewed interest. Also during this time, the U.S. National Park Service prepared a report on the ships that included detailed drawings, photographs, and videotapes.

Even with all of the recent research, many of the ships have yet to be positively identified because most of the nameplates were removed during initial salvage operations. In some cases the only remaining clues to their identity lie in a serial number on a boiler buried deep in the engine room or on an insignia found on a broken piece of pottery.

Not all of the wrecks are safe to dive. One is lying upside down and is dangerous to enter. Some have been so blown apart that they are now only twisted hulks of metal scattered about the lagoon floor. But some of the ships have been transformed into living reefs magnificently adorned with forests of black coral, delicate sea fans, and schools of fish. And several ships known to have sunk in Palau that have yet to be located.

Most of the ships lie in the protected waters of the Palau Lagoon, just ten to fifteen minutes from Koror by boat. Many can be seen without diving deeper than one hundred feet. All are protected under the Palau Lagoon Monument Act. It is illegal to remove anything from the ships. Four of the most popular wrecks are detailed on the following pages.

Preceding page: An attack photo taken on March 30, 1944, shows Japanese ships on fire and sinking. The ship at the top of the photograph, just left of the center margin, is the <u>Amatsu Maru</u>. The ship with smoke billowing from her engine room, bottom center of photograph, is the <u>Iro</u>. Photograph courtesy of the US National Archives 80-G-45323

IRO

CLASS:	FLEET OIL TANKER
LENGTH:	470 FEET
WEIGHT:	14,050 TONS
DEPTH:	80 FEET TO DECK
	120 FEET TO BOTTOM
POSITION:	UPRIGHT
HEADING:	NORTHEAST

On March 30, 1944, the 470-foot Japanese tanker *Iro* was hit by a bomb near her engine room and slowly sank to the bottom of the Palau Lagoon. Today, nearly half a century later, this vestige of war has been transformed into a living monument to the endurance of nature. Hard and soft corals have overgrown much of the ship. Schools of jacks and fusiliers patrol the now-vacant corridors. Curious batfish follow divers as they explore the wreck. Even several giant clams are living on top of the ship's center mast—precariously balanced forty-five feet above the main deck. The abundance of marine life together with the interesting features of this ship have made the *Iro* the most popular wreck dive in Palau.

The *Iro* lies upright in eighty to 120 feet of water on the west side of Ngeruktabel Island in an area of the Palau Lagoon where visibility can range from twenty-five feet to more than sixty. Her forward king posts (the vertical masts used to support the equipment that loaded and unloaded cargo) rise to within twenty-five feet of the surface and are packed with mussels, fluted oysters, and bright red encrusting sponges. Huge 5.5-inch guns, heavily

The Iro slowly sinks to the bottom of the lagoon. Although most of the damage to the ship was in the engine room at the stern, a skip bomb blew a hole in the bow, clearly visible in this photograph. Photograph courtesy of the US National Archives 80-G-45321

encrusted with coral, still remain on both the bow and the stern.

The ship was anchored at the time she sank, and her coral-encrusted anchor chain still hangs from the starboard bow. Large bushes of black coral now partially camouflage the huge gaping hole where a skip bomb blew away a piece of the bow.

The bridge is open and easy to explore, but most of the ship's instruments are missing and have presumably been salvaged. At the stern, the engine room is wide open and easy to enter, but it looks like a room full of twisted metal unless you are familiar with coal- or oil-fired steam engines. The Nippon Salvage Company was never successful in its attempts to remove the enormous brass propeller. Today it lies partially buried in the silt at 120 feet.

Although this ship has been called the *Iro* for years, there is still some question as to its actual identity. It is possible that this is the wreck of her sister ship, the *Sata*, which also sank in this area. The only difference between the two was the type of boilers used in the engine rooms. For now it is impossible to positively identify either ship since one ship lies dangerously inverted, and this ship, currently identified as the *Iro,* has been heavily damaged in the engine room. Until further identification efforts, it is presumed that this is the wreck of the *Iro.*

The Iro, *built in 1922, was nearly twenty years old by the time she sank, but she was a valuable ship for the Japanese. She served as a fleet oil tanker and was rigged to refuel ships at sea. Her rusting hull is now overgrown with marine life.* Photograph by Rick Tegeler

AMATSU MARU

CLASS:	**TANKER**
LENGTH:	**527 FEET**
WEIGHT:	**10,567 TONS**
DEPTH:	**80 FEET TO BRIDGE**
	100 FEET TO MAIN DECK
	130 FEET TO BOTTOM
POSITION:	**UPRIGHT**
HEADING:	**NORTHEAST**

The *Amatsu Maru* is the largest shipwreck in Palau, so large that the serious wreck diver will want more than one dive to explore it completely. Her enormous 530-foot-long hull is intact and covered with one of the largest known forests of black coral in Palau. Locally the ship is known as The Black Coral Wreck. According to Klaus Lindemann, this is one of the classic wreck dives of the world, comparable to many of the world-class wrecks of the famous Truk Lagoon.

The *Amatsu Maru* was a civilian oil tanker built in 1943 during Japan's emergency shipbuilding program for the war. She was specifically designed to outrun American submarines, which had been taking a heavy toll on the Japanese ships that were supplying their homeland with crude oil to sustain the war effort. Japanese ships that carry the suffix "maru" are civilian or merchant marine ships. Maru can be translated to mean "safe journey" or "round-trip," implying to get there and back. The *Amatsu Maru,* however, never made it back. Today she lies on the bottom of the Palau Lagoon.

The ship was anchored in Malakal Harbor, just south of Ngarol Island,

Soft corals and fluted oysters grow from the rusting hulls of many of the ships in Palau.
Photograph by Rick Tegeler

at the time she sank. She now lies upright in one hundred to 130 feet of water just ten minutes from Koror by boat. Visibility on this wreck is rarely much more than sixty feet, which adds an eerie quality to the ship's ghostly remains. Her king posts reach to within forty feet of the surface and are so thickly coated with mussels and oysters that many of the shells have lost their footing and have fallen to the decks below. Her main deck lies between ninety and one hundred feet and is covered with a heavy layer of sediment, so use care not to stir up the silt. The front of the ship is overgrown with black coral—the forward face of the bridge is a living wall of black coral trees, some eight to ten feet tall. Red snapper and skip jack school at the bow of the ship, and lionfish hover in the shadows of the rusting hull.

Most of the interior wooden decks of the bridge have disintegrated, so the area is open and easy to explore. Inside, the remains of the ship's radio room can be seen, and Japanese commodes lie scattered among the loose wiring and debris.

The stern has been heavily damaged and is now a confusing array of tumbled grated walkways and fallen metal support beams. There is a small hole (about fifteen inches across) located just forward of the engine room, about ten feet to starboard of the ship's centerline, which is believed to have been made by the bomb that sank the ship. It appears that the bomb penetrated at least two or three decks before it detonated as the topside damage is minimal. Another strong explosion blew a large hole (about thirty by forty-five feet in diameter) on top of the engine room, allowing easy access to the area. Entry is not advised, however, because of the tangled mass of hanging cables and fallen machinery.

At the stern the enormous propeller lies in 110 to 120 feet of water. Its four massive blades have a diameter of over sixteen feet—an impressive sight in the dim light at this depth.

Black coral and oysters decorate an open hatch on the Amatsu Maru. Photograph by Mitchell P. Warner

GOZAN MARU

CLASS:	**MERCHANT SHIP**
LENGTH:	**390 FEET**
DEPTH:	**50-60 FEET TO STARBOARD RAIL**
	100 FEET TO PORTSIDE RAIL
POSITION:	**HEAVY LIST TO PORT**
HEADING:	**EAST**

An intriguing thing about diving wrecks in Palau is that some of the ships have yet to be identified. Such is the case with this wreck, which for years was thought to be the *Hokutai Maru*. After an extensive study in 1987, ship historian Klaus Lindemann determined that this is instead the *Gozan Maru*. But there is currently a spirited debate between researchers as to its actual identity.

The ship was anchored off the western shores of Ngeruktabel Island at the time it sank—so close to shore that while sinking it rolled to port and slid down the foot of the island. It finally came to rest on the one-hundred-foot-deep sand bottom, listing heavily to port with the bow facing east toward the island.

The starboard deck rests in fifty to sixty feet of water, making this one of the more shallow wreck dives in Palau, but visibility can be poor in this area so the ship is not often dived. An immense hole made by the bomb that sank the ship is located on the starboard hull between sixty and seventy feet, just forward of the bridge. The bridge itself is open and easy to enter, but exploring it can be disorientating because of the severe list of the ship. The helm and engine telegraph still remain inside the bridge, but both instruments have fallen to port and are now so overgrown with coral that they are almost unrecognizable. At the stern, rusting pots and pans lie scattered about the galley, along with Japanese china, some inscribed with an insignia that might hold the only clue to the true identity of this ship.

A diver prepares to enter the ship's bridge. Photograph by Mitchell P. Warner

THE BUOY NO. 6 WRECK

CLASS:	**JAPANESE FISHING BOAT**
LENGTH:	**80 FEET**
DEPTH:	**70 FEET TO DECK**
	80 FEET TO BOTTOM
POSITION:	**UPRIGHT**
HEADING:	**NORTHWEST**

A Japanese fishing boat that was sunk during the war lies upright in eighty feet of water in Lighthouse Channel, also known as Malakal Passage. Because it is located near buoy marker no. 6, the wreck is simply referred to as The Buoy No.6 Wreck. At one time the ship was fitted with a small bow gun, which has since been removed, so it is likely that during the war it was used not only for fishing but as a submarine chaser as well.

The Buoy No.6 Wreck is a pretty dive. Even though the ship is small, it is covered with a lush growth of coral, making it a popular dive with photographers. The pilot house is overflowing with sea fans and soft corals, and an unusual variety of "white" black coral grows from the rusting hull. The forward hold is small but open and large enough to swim through. Inside, divers are often surrounded by a school of silvery bait fish. At night the ship blooms with basket stars, orange tube corals, and the expanded polyps of feeding corals making this wreck a popular area for night dives.

Lighthouse Channel is a busy area for small boat traffic, so stay to the side of the channel when you surface. Also, because this wreck lies in a channel, be prepared for strong currents.

Lionfish, Pterois volitans, hover in the dark corridors of the coral-encrusted decks.
Photograph by Rick Tegeler

HAZARDOUS MARINE LIFE

*S*urvival in the marine environment depends not only on an animal's ability to capture food, but also on its ability to defend itself. To eat or to be eaten is the reality of life on the reef. The feeding and defensive mechanisms of many marine animals are just as effective against humans as they are against natural predators and prey. Knowledge of an animal's behavior and respect for its environment are the best ways to avoid a potentially dangerous situation. The following pages describe a few of the marine animals in Palau that divers should be aware of.

Preceding page: Oceanic white tip sharks, <u>Carcharhinus longimanus</u>, are very aggressive open-ocean predators. They are sometimes seen around the islands of Peleliu, Angaur, and Kayangel. Photograph by Al Giddings

As the name implies, fire coral, <u>Millepora sp.</u>, can cause a burning pain, similar to that caused by an open flame. Photograph by Rick Tegeler

FIRE CORAL

Fire coral causes a burning pain when brushed with bare skin. While it looks like a "true" hard coral because of its calcareous skeleton, fire coral is more closely related to the infamous Portuguese man-of-war.

Fire coral encrusts other surfaces, thereby taking on many shapes, from branching fingerlike projections to flat platelike formations. Its distinguishing features are its dull mustard-brown color, white tips, and fine hairlike polyps that extend from its surface. These polyps are adapted for feeding as well as for defense and contain nematocysts, microscopic stinging capsules that can inject irritating toxins into the skin. The resulting burning sensation usually disappears in a few hours, but red welts may appear.

If you are stung by fire coral, do not rub the affected area as this will cause any nematocysts that remain on the skin to inject more toxin. First rinse the area with vinegar to inactivate the nematocysts. Then thoroughly wash the wound with soap and water. Hydrocortisone cream relieves the itching.

These delicate looking and seemingly harmless animals known as hydroids can sting bare skin. Most hydroid stings are mild and considered nothing more than a nuisance by many divers. Photograph by Rick Tegeler

HYDROIDS

Hydroids are stationary colonies of small animals that look like plants. They vary in appearance from delicate featherlike clusters to sturdier plantlike ferns and typically grow no taller than eight inches. They are found on most of the reefs in Palau and on many of the wrecks, ranging in color from neutral shades of gray or brown to striking black stalks with silver fronds.

Hydroids contain nematocysts, potent stinging capsules that cause a burning pain when touched. Intensity of the sting depends not only on the kind of hydroid encountered, but also on the number of nematocysts injected and the sensitivity of the person stung. Most stings are mild, and the pain usually disappears quickly. But red welts or blisters often appear on the skin, and an annoying rash usually develops. Stings should be treated by first rinsing the affected area in vinegar to disable any nematocysts that remain on the skin. Apply hydrocortisone cream, such as Cortaid, to relieve the itching.

Long-spined sea urchins, such as the species of <u>Diadema</u> pictured here, are covered with needle-sharp spines, which they use for protection against certain reef fish that consider them a delicacy. Photograph by Ed Robinson

SEA URCHINS

Although most sea urchins are harmless to divers, the long-spined sea urchin is covered with needle-sharp spines that can easily pierce a wetsuit. Hidden within these spines, which vary in length from two to twelve inches, are smaller secondary spines coated with a venomous mucus that causes even further discomfort from puncture wounds.

Sea urchins generally hide in crevices, under ledges, or in caves during the day and are easy to avoid. If you happen to receive a puncture wound, try to remove as many of the embedded spines as possible and soak the affected area in hot water (120° to 130° F) for thirty to ninety minutes to detoxify the venom and alleviate the pain. Sea urchin spines are brittle and often break off when grabbed with tweezers, making them difficult to remove completely. Any small fragments that remain in the skin will eventually dissolve or fester and be rejected, but this may take several weeks.

Stout spines coated with a venomous mucus cover the body of the aptly named crown of thorns starfish, <u>Acanthaster planci</u>. These starfish can grow as many as twenty-three arms, but the average number is sixteen. Photograph by Mitchell P. Warner

CROWN OF THORNS STARFISH

The infamous reputation of the crown of thorns starfish, *Acanthaster planci*, comes more from its ability to destroy a coral reef than from its potential hazard to divers. An army of these starfish can turn a coral garden into a graveyard of bleached skeletons within days. Nevertheless, divers should be aware that these starfish are covered with stout spines coated with a venomous mucus. Because of the potency of this venom, a puncture wound can cause pain and swelling in excess of that expected from the injury alone.

The crown of thorns is nocturnal and often hides deep within the coral heads by day. During certain cyclical periods, however, they feed twenty-four hours a day and are out on the reef at all times, which increases the chance of injury to divers. Wounds should be treated by removing all pieces of embedded spines and soaking the area in hot water (120° to 130° F) for thirty to ninety minutes to detoxify the venom.

Pictured above are a few of the potentially dangerous cone shells found in Palau. Clockwise from upper left: Conus striatus, C. omaria, C. geographus (responsible for the most human fatalities), C. aulicus, C. tulipa, C. marmoreus, and C. textile. Photograph by Sam Sargent

CONE SHELLS

The ornate, attractive patterns found on cone shells make them a favorite among shell collectors throughout the world. But cone shells get their revenge. Several of the more than 400 species possess a highly toxic venom that has caused human fatalities.

Cone shells are carnivorous and kill their prey by shooting a poisonous dart through a retractable tubular mouth called a proboscis. Even though the proboscis is located at the narrow end of the shell, it is able to reach around and sting a hand holding the shell's large, broad end.

Most cone shell stings are not fatal, but it is often difficult to identify individual species because of a layer of brown tissue that covers many of the shells. Consequently, all cone shells should be regarded with caution. If you are stung by a cone shell, any cone shell, securely wrap the wound and seek medical attention immediately.

*Hidden within the delicate feathery plumage of the lionfish (*Pterois antennata* pictured here) are long, needle-sharp spines that can inject a highly toxic venom.* Photograph by Mitchell P. Warner

LIONFISH

Lionfish are among the most beautiful fish on the reef—attracting the attention of divers and photographers alike. But be aware that hidden within their delicate feathery plumage are long, needle-sharp spines that can inject a highly toxic venom. Although this venom is usually not lethal to humans, it can cause excruciating pain.

Fortunately, you have to work hard to get stung by a lionfish. They are often found under ledges or clinging to the inside walls of caves during the day, although at times they swim openly on the reef. Lionfish will not attack unless provoked, but if they feel threatened, they lower their heads and charge, spines first, making quick jabbing movements in the direction of the threat.

The active ingredient in the venom of a lionfish is a protein that is broken down by heat. Wounds should be soaked in very hot, but not scalding, water (120° to 130° F) for thirty to ninety minutes or until the pain disappears.

Stonefish, such as this <u>Synanceja verrucosa</u>, are the masters of camouflage as they lie motionless on the bottom waiting to prey upon small fish or a tennis shoe that ventures too close. Photograph by Brian Gibeson

STONEFISH

The stonefish, *Synanceja sp.*, has one of the most deadly reputations on the reef. Hidden among its warty skin are thirteen dorsal spines that can inject a highly toxic venom when touched or stepped on. Although puncture wounds are rarely fatal, they can cause agonizing, almost unbearable, pain for hours.

Stonefish, as the name implies, look like a rock or coral-covered stone. Because they lie motionless under rocks or partially buried in the sand, they almost disappear within the reef. Most injuries occur when people accidently step on them—when disturbed, this fearless fish simply holds its ground and erects its dorsal spines. Tennis shoes or heavy-soled diving booties offer protection when walking in the water.

Stonefish wounds are treated with heat. Soak the wound in hot water (120° to 130° F) for thirty to ninety minutes or until you get to the hospital. Victims may go into shock, so seek medical attention as soon as possible.

Grey reef sharks, <u>Carcharhinus amblyrhynchos</u>, which can grow to seven feet in length, are the most aggressive of the sharks commonly found on Palauan reefs. The distinguishing feature of these sharks is the black trailing edge to the tail fin. Photograph by Rick Tegeler

SHARKS

The land sharks in Palau are far more aggressive than the marine species. They are nocturnal and generally feed around the local bars in Koror.

Underwater, there are two types of sharks divers encounter, free-swimming and bottom-dwelling. Bottom-dwelling sharks, such as leopard and nurse sharks, are generally harmless unless harassed by divers. It is the free-swimming varieties that cause the greatest anxiety.

Almost all tropical species of sharks are found in Palau, but the ones most often seen by divers are whitetips, *Triaenodon obesus;* blacktips, *Carcharhinus melanopterus;* and grey reef sharks, *Carcharhinus amblyrhynchos.* Although all sharks should be regarded with caution, most reef sharks that frequent the popular dive sites in Palau are accustomed to divers and present little danger as long as there is no spear fishing in the area.

Blacktip reef sharks have distinctive black tips on their fins. Although

Whitetip reef shark, Triaenodon obesus. Photograph by Ed Robinson

they grow as large as six feet and may be inquisitive, they tend to be shy and easily frightened by divers.

Whitetip reef sharks have an obvious white tip on their dorsal and tail fins. These curious yet generally nonaggressive sharks pose little threat to divers unless they are provoked. Unlike most other sharks, which must swim constantly to keep oxygen-supplying water over their gills, the whitetip reef shark can pump water over its gills while it remains motionless on the bottom. Whitetips are often found resting on flat, sandy areas of the reef or in caves to which they regularly return.

Grey reef sharks are the most territorial of the sharks commonly found on Palauan reefs. When threatened they display a distinctive aggressive posture — arched back, nose up, tail down — a clear warning to get out of their way. Schools of grey reef sharks may readily enter into a feeding frenzy when bait or speared fish are in the water. If you are concerned about sharks, do not chase them and do not spear fish. No unprovoked shark attacks are known to have occurred in Palau.

Unlike other sea snakes, the banded sea snake, <u>Laticauda colubrina</u>, can move about as easily on land as in the water. It is not uncommon to see them in the Rock Islands sunning on ledges near the water. Photograph by Ed Robinson

SEA SNAKES

There are more than fifty species of sea snakes in the world, but the banded sea snake, *Laticauda colubrina*, is the one most often seen in Palau. Its silver body is marked with jet-black bands and a pale yellow snout. Although curious, these snakes are generally nonaggressive and rarely attempt to bite, even when provoked. Their venom, however, is more toxic than that of a cobra, and bites have been fatal.

Sea snakes breathe air, but are able to stay submerged for over an hour as they hunt around coral heads for food. They paralyze their prey by injecting venom through grooved fangs located in the back of their mouth. Because the mouth is small, many sea snakes are not able to obtain a wide enough bite to pierce wetsuits. Their fangs can also break off easily, which frequently results in bites without envenomization. Nevertheless, a bite from a sea snake is a medical emergency requiring immediate medical attention.

Don't be fooled by those crocodile tears. Behind that sinister smile is a reptile that survived the great extinction of the dinosaurs more than 65 million years ago. Although crocodiles are an endangered species today, their numbers have increased dramatically in some areas because of recent years of protection. Fortunately, the population in Palau remains small.

CROCODILES

There are two species of crocodiles in Palau, the saltwater crocodile, *Crocodylus porosus,* and the freshwater New Guinea crocodile, *C. noveaguinae.* Both live in the mangrove swamps around Babeldaob and have also been seen in some of the marine lakes of the Rock Islands. Crocodiles are not found on the offshore reefs where most of the dive sites are located, and because they are generally nocturnal, it is unlikely that divers will see them in the wild.

Saltwater crocodiles can live for seventy years and grow to an impressive length of twenty feet, although average size is between twelve and fifteen feet. They are carnivores from the moment they hatch from their nests. Adults feed on turtles, fish, birds, and mammals, although their only criteria for a good meal is being able to catch it. They are excellent swimmers, extremely fast on their feet, and are capable of inflicting a lethal blow with their tails.

CONSERVATION

*T*he Palauan people have a connection to the ocean that few outsiders understand. From their early creation legends, it was the sea that gave them life, and it will be the sea that sustains them in years to come.

Conservation is not new in Palau. For centuries traditional laws regulated the marine environment so that there would be food for future generations. It was illegal to fish certain reefs during spawning season, and many marine animals were allowed to be taken only for village chiefs or for certain marriage or childbirth ceremonies. The laws were obeyed out of fear of punishment or death.

Today there has been a breakdown of these traditional laws. Even though modern laws now regulate the taking of many marine species, poaching still continues due to lack of money for enforcement.

Many Palauans are strict conservationists and are doing their best to protect their environment. Yet as the popularity of the islands increases, they have an ever more difficult task. Ironically, tourism often destroys the very thing that attracts it. Today divers are increasingly aware of the damage that can occur when reefs are dived again and again. The reefs of Palau are some of the most beautiful in the world. As visitors to these islands, we must respect Palau's fragile marine ecosystem. Leave the reefs as you found them so that others may enjoy them for many years to come.

Rick Tegeler

THINGS TO DO, PEOPLE TO SEE

*I*f you decide to take a day off from diving, there are a number of places in town worth a visit. One recommendation is the Micronesian Mariculture Demonstration Center (MMDC). The MMDC is a research laboratory and hatchery engaged in the cultivation of commercially important species. Their main research project and success story involves the giant tridacnid clam. The clam has been a favorite seafood among Pacific Islanders since ancient times, but recent massive commercial exploitation by foreign poachers, mainly Taiwanese, has nearly wiped out these molluscs. Researchers at the MMDC have developed a method of breeding tridacnids in captivity, and the center now sells seed clams to countries throughout the Pacific as part of a program to re-establish the nearly extinct clam population.

Another project at the center is a hawksbill turtle hatchery, which has been in operation for nearly five years. Tagged turtles from the MMDC nursery have recently been recaptured in Guam and the Philippines, which indicates high mobility of the released hatchlings. The center is open from 8:00 a.m. to 4:00 p.m. weekdays and charges a modest admission fee. Tanks full of tridacnid clams with iridescent multicolored mantles are on display, along with hawksbill, green, and loggerhead turtles. All are endangered species.

In front of the MMDC, just to the left of the cement steps, is a rich, shallow fringing reef that is an ideal site for snorkeling. Plans are currently underway to establish a "snorkeling trail" in this area with numbered buoys and printed trail guides identifying the different species of marine life. On the way to the reef, snorkelers swim over what looks like a giant clam plantation, rows and rows of neatly spaced flats filled with young clams bred by the center.

For a glimpse into Palau's past, the Belau National Museum offers artifacts and exhibits of early Palauan culture, including the head of a fourteen-foot crocodile. Many of the oldest and best examples of well-crafted Palauan artifacts were taken from the country by anthropologists at the turn of the century and are now displayed in German and British museums. But the exhibits at the Palau museum are the best collection in this part of the world, and they help give the visitor a better understanding of this country's fascinating history. The museum is open from 8:00 to 11:00 a.m. and 1:00 to 4:00 p.m. weekdays and from 10:00 a.m. to 2:00 p.m. on Saturday. There is a nominal admission fee.

One of the most unusual places in town to visit is the local jail, where inmates sell storyboards, carved planks of wood depicting early Palauan legends. Many of the prisoners are very talented artists who carve storyboards of the highest quality. Prices are negotiable. Visiting hours are from 1:00 to 3:30 p.m. daily.

For those who don't feel like braving the prison yard, there are two excellent carvers who work in the open-air summer house next to the museum. If you can't find your favorite legend for sale elsewhere, either carver will make special order storyboards and ship them to you.

The Palauan postage stamps are becoming collectors items with a small but growing number of tourists. They can be purchased from the local post office, located in the center of town. First-day issues and out-of-print stamps can also be purchased at the Shopping Center and Desekel Market, two of the local stores.

Tortoiseshell jewelry is also for sale, but it is illegal to take tortoiseshell products into many countries, the United States included, because the hawksbill turtle from which the jewelry is made is an endangered species.

The best selection of woven handbags, hats, and betel nut bags can be found at the Senior Citizens Center, where women gather in the open-air summer house to weave. The center is open from 7:30 a.m. to 4:30 p.m. weekdays.

The only remaining traditional *bai* in Palau is located in Airai state, about a thirty-minute drive from Koror. The *bai* is an important symbol of Micronesian history, and many of the traditional skills used in its construction are slowly disappearing. The Airai Bai was built in 1889 and has withstood a century of typhoons and deterioration by termites and rot, testimony to its solid construction. Historically, most *bais* lasted only fifty years. Today the Airai Bai is a combination museum and community hall. It is still an integral part of the life of the villagers, and proper conduct includes a quiet, respectful attitude. There is an admission charge for viewing the *bai*, with additional fees charged for still or video photography.

Also in Airai, there is a crocodile farm just across the street from the Mobil gas station. There is no sign—go through the laundromat to pay the small admission fee. This may be your only chance to see a live saltwater crocodile, and these crocodiles are big, a few are nearly ten feet long.

Palau is breathtaking when seen from the air. Paradise Air, the local airline, offers daily flights to the southern islands of Peleliu and Angaur. The round-trip takes less than two hours and provides an unforgettable view of the Rock Islands and the Ngemelis area dive sites. Planes can also be chartered for sightseeing tours of the northern island of Kayangel.

As for nightlife, bars come and go in Palau, but there are ample places to quench your thirst, and most clubs offer live entertainment. There is also a midnight curfew so it's hard to get into too much trouble.

The rooster, herald of the sun and a symbol of commerce, appeared on every <u>bai</u>, *the traditional men's meeting house. The bird was always pictured sitting on a semicircle set against a black background — the black background representing night and the semicircle illustrating the rising sun. The circle with a cross design is the symbol for Palauan money.*

KNOW BEFORE YOU GO

*I*t takes forever to get to Palau from the United States. Actual flying time from the west coast is fourteen hours, but plane changes in Honolulu and Guam add several more hours of travel time. You cross the International Date Line during the trip so you lose a day on the way over and pick up a day on your return. The most convenient airline connections to Palau from the United States are provided by Continental and Continental Air Micronesia (call toll-free from the United States 1-800-231-0856). Travelers originating from Pacific Rim countries will make connections in Guam, Japan, or the Philippines. There are no direct flights from Europe to Palau. Connections can be made through Honolulu, Hong Kong, Tokyo, or Manila. Continental Air Micronesia provides the only continuing service into Koror from these connecting points.

ENTRY REQUIREMENTS: For entry, U.S. citizens must have proof of citizenship: a passport, birth certificate, or voter registration card. Non-U.S. citizens need a valid passport. All visitors must show a return ticket or a ticket to a further destination. Return reservations should be reconfirmed seventy-two hours before departure, and there is a small departure tax. If your stay is going to exceed thirty days, you must obtain a visa from the Palauan Immigration Office upon arrival.

IMMUNIZATIONS: No vaccinations are required if your travel originates in the United States. Small-pox immunization is mandatory if you are entering Palau from any country except the United States, and immunization against cholera and yellow fever is required if you're arriving from an infected area.

LANGUAGE: Palauan is the national language, but English is the official language and is spoken by almost everyone on the island.

CURRENCY: The U.S. dollar is the only currency, and major credit cards are accepted in most hotels and several dive shops.

ELECTRICITY: Electricity is 110 volts, 60 cycle, the same as in the United States.

WATER: The water system in Palau is currently being replaced. Local residents drink fresh rainwater or boil tap water for ten minutes. Major hotels and restaurants have their own water filtering systems, and their tap water is safe to drink.

HOTELS: Hotel accommodations range from the luxurious Palau Pacific Resort, located on the only beach in Koror, to the comfortable DW Motel (a favorite with divers), conveniently located in the center of town. A popular medium-priced hotel is The Hotel Nikko Palau, an older hotel built into a beautifully landscaped hillside overlooking some of the Rock Islands. At the time of this writing, there are additional hotels nearing completion. For further information contact the Palau Tourist Authority, Box 256, Koror, Republic of Palau, 96940.

TRANSPORTATION: Transportation from the airport, which is about a fifteen-minute drive from the center of the main town of Koror, is provided by bus or taxi. Several of the smaller hotels will send someone to meet you at the airport if previous arrangements have been made. All dive operators offer free transportation to their dive shops from any hotel. Rental cars are available in Koror, and most companies accept major credit cards, but not all of them offer insurance.

WEATHER: Temperatures range from the mid-70s° F in the evenings to the high 80s° F midday. Humidity averages a steamy eighty-two percent, but the cool, gentle trade winds provide refreshing relief. As a general rule, Palau has a wet summer and a dry winter. Average yearly rainfall is nearly 150 inches, so expect light rain showers almost daily. The wet summer months—June, July, and August—each average fifteen inches of rain. But the driest months—February, March, and April—still receive about eight inches of rain monthly.

CLOTHING: The heat, humidity, and relaxed pace of the islands call for light-weight casual clothing. Beachwear is not appropriate in town, and if you visit a village outside of Koror, Palauan culture suggests that women wear a knee-length skirt, dress, or wrap.

BUSINESS HOURS: Stores are open from 7:30 a.m. to 8:00 p.m. Many of the retail shops are closed on Saturdays and open on Sundays. The Post Office is open from 7:30 a.m. to 4:30 p.m. Monday through Friday. Banks are open from 9:00 a.m. to 3:30 p.m. weekdays.

TIPPING: Tipping for services rendered is not customary, but is appreciated.

TIME: The Palau Islands are nine hours ahead of Greenwich Mean Time. Twelve o'clock noon in Palau is also 12:00 noon in Tokyo, 11:00 a.m. in Manila, 1:00 p.m. in Sydney, and 7:00 p.m. Pacific Standard Time the previous day in California.

HOTEL ADDRESSES: DW Motel, Box 738, Koror, Palau 96940, Telex 728-1725; Hotel Nikko Palau, Box 310, Koror, Palau 96940, Phone 486, Telex 728-8938; Palau Pacific Resort, Box 308, Koror, Palau 96940, Phone 600, Telex 728-8920, Fax 1601.

DIVE SHOPS: Aqua Pro, Box 37, Koror, Palau 96940, Phone 1232;
Blue Marlin, Box 669, Koror, Palau 96940, Phone 583;
Fish 'N Fins, Box 142, Koror, Palau 96940, Phone 637;
Neco Marine, Box 129, Koror, Palau 96940, Phone 1755;
New World Dive & Sail Charters, 1216, Koror, Palau 96940, Phone 1363;
Palau Diving Center, Box 5, Koror, Palau 96940, Phone 978;
Sam Scott's Underwater Tours, Box 428, Koror, Palau 96940, Phone 1471;
Splash, Box 847, Koror, Palau 96940, Phone 600.

SUGGESTED READINGS

HISTORY

An Account of the Pelew Islands, by George Keate, 1788; A fascinating although somewhat idealized account of the first recorded contact between Europeans and Palauans—the shipwreck of British Captain Henry Wilson. The book became a popular play in England at the turn of the century. This extremely old volume is difficult to find; try the rare book section of the library.

A History of Palau, Volumes I, II, and III, edited by Kathryn Kesoli, The Palau Community Action Agency, 1976; An excellent history of Palau written and produced by Palauans. These three volumes are now out-of-print and may be difficult to find.

The First Taint of Civilization, by Francis X. Hezel SJ (University of Hawaii Press, Honolulu, 1983); An excellent history of Micronesia during the pre-colonial era from 1521 to 1885, written by a long-time resident.

ENVIRONMENT

A Field Guide to the Birds of Hawaii and the Tropical Pacific, by H. Douglas Pratt, Phillip L. Bruner and Delwyn G. Barrett (Princeton University Press, 1987); A useful reference to Pacific Island birds, written for the serious birder and the novice alike. The book includes color illustrations of each species of bird that breeds in the Tropical Pacific, as well as those that migrate through the area.

Field Guide to the Birds of Palau, by John Enbring, prepared by the Conservation

Office in cooperation with the Bureau of Education, Koror, Palau, 1988; An easy-to-use guide for identifying the fifty resident species of birds in Palau and some of the more common migrants. The book features charming color illustrations and includes the Palauan name for each species as well as several local legends about birds.

This Living Reef, by Douglas Faulkner (Quadrangle, The New York Times Company, New York, 1971); A handsome coffee-table book by well-known underwater photographer and environmentalist Douglas Faulkner. This classic volume includes insightful commentary and color photographs of the Palauan reefs from the early 1970s, before scuba diving became popular in the islands. Faulkner was one of the first underwater photographers to capture Palau on film, and the book drew international attention to the islands.

Micronesian Reef Fishes, by Robert F. Meyers (Coral Graphics, Box 21153, GMF, Barrigada, Guam 96921, USA, 1989); An invaluable guide for identifying many of the fish found in Micronesia. The book includes color photographs and descriptions of the behavior of each species.

GENERAL

A Reporter in Micronesia, by E.J. Kahn (W.W. Norton Co., New York, 1966); A witty account of a reporter's adventures through Micronesia in the early 1960s, before commercial airline flights and tourists hit the area.

A Song for Satawal, by Kenneth Brower (Penguin Books, 1983); A story of three local inhabitants of the islands of Yap, Saipan, and Palau and their efforts to preserve a part of their islands' history and culture.

The Palau Islands, by Mandy Thyssen (Neco Tours and Neco Marine Dive Shop, Box 129, Koror, Palau 96940, 1988); Written by a former dive guide in Palau who now makes her home in the islands, the book is an informative look at the people, culture, history, diving, and flora and fauna through text, color photographs, and beautiful line illustrations.

Micronesia: The Land, the People and the Sea, by Kenneth Brower (Louisiana State University Press, Baton Rouge and London, 1981); The relationship Micronesians have to the sea is shown through text and color photographs. The book includes interesting sections on canoes, fishing, and navigation.

Micronesian Customs and Beliefs, by The Students of The Community College of Micronesia, compiled and edited by Gene Ashby (Rainy Day Press, Box 3035, Eugene, OR 97403, Second Edition, 1985); A charming, easy-to-read book about traditional Micronesian customs, written by local students.

With Their Islands Around Them, by Kenneth Brower (Holt, Rinehart and Winston, New York, 1974); The story of two men, a Palauan and an American living in Palau, and their efforts to preserve the natural resources of the islands. Written by a man with a keen sense of observation and subtle sense of humor, the book so beautifully captures the essence of life in Palau that reading it is almost like being there. Highly recommended.

Words of the Lagoon, by R.E. Johannes (University of California Press, Berkeley and Los Angeles, 1981); An excellent book about traditional fishing methods and marine lore of Palau, written by a marine biologist who substantiated much of the traditional knowledge of Palauan fishermen with scientific fact.

SHIPWRECKS

Desecrate 1, The Shipwrecks of Palau, by Klaus Lindemann (Pacific Press Publications, 318 Brain Avenue, Belleville, MI 48111, 1988); A detailed description of the shipwrecks in the Palau lagoon, including locations, types, measurements and silhouettes of each of the Japanese ships that were sunk in Palau during World War II.

Ed Robinson